Facing Life's Challenges with Confidence and Hope

———◇———

P.O. Box 799070
Dallas, TX 75379
1-800-414-7693
jgraham@powerpoint.org
www.jackgraham.org

All rights reserved
by Jack Graham
Printed in the United States of America

Unless otherwise noted, all Scripture quotations are from The Holy Bible: English Standard Version.
Copyright© 2011, Crossway. Used by permission.

TABLE OF CONTENTS

Introduction		I
I.	Help! I'm Afraid	1
II.	Help! I'm Stressed	20
III.	Help! I'm Addicted	40
IV.	Help! I'm Lonely	57
V.	Help! I'm Grieving	76
VI.	Help! I'm Angry	95
VII.	Help! I'm Depressed	113
VIII.	Help! I'm Tempted	131
IX.	Help! I'm Filled With Shame	152
Final Thoughts		174

INTRODUCTION

In the fall of 2019, I felt God calling me to deliver sermons on issues you rarely hear discussed from pulpits in our nation. Topics that make people uncomfortable. Subject matter that 15 years ago, no one was really preaching on. Problems I might have addressed as asides to a "larger" message, but ones toward which I hadn't dedicated a whole message. But I felt the urgency, the need, and the desperation of my congregation to deliver a sermon series singularly and directly on these topics. They involve mental and emotional health issues such as fear, addiction, stress, grief, anger, temptation, depression, loneliness, and shame.

These issues are something I know about, having loved people who had struggled with them, or having repeatedly seen throughout my years of counseling. I began preparation for each sermon on my knees in prayer and at my keyboard in research. That sermon series was called *Help: Facing Life's Challenges with Confidence and Hope*.

I can honestly say I have rarely seen and heard such a

heart-felt response to any series I have preached. It was not due to any particular expertise I had in these areas of struggle, but due to the Holy Spirit beginning a healing in His people. And in addition to God's good work and the open hearts and prayers of my congregation, I attribute the success of this series to two reasons.

The first is we are living in a pressure-cooker world like never before. Anyone can observe never before seen levels of stress, anger, and unhappiness in our culture. Social media and the news are filled daily with examples of the brokenness of people's lives. This is being expressed in the streets, on the comment boards, in the shootings, and in the arguments and agitation in our communities. I can tell you that as a pastor of four-plus decades, I have never seen so much brokenness, emotional and mental struggles, and pain in peoples' lives as we are seeing today.

The second reason is that those who are suffering from depression, fear, anxiety, addiction, and other mental and emotional health issues no longer feel the ungodly stigma which forced them into the shadows. Television talk shows, writers, academics, the medical community, and even Hollywood celebrities have actually helped our culture by studying, talking about, and reporting on these issues, such that the stigma of suffering has been diminished. People now seek treatment and help, regardless of the consequences to their "image." The high-profile, A-list movie star seeking help and speaking about her depression or addiction seems to have benefited the "soccer mom" who can't seem to get through the day's stresses without a pill, a glass of wine, or lashing out in frustrated anger at her family. People are finally understanding that it's okay to admit to not being okay and then seeking help. While previous generations, particularly Christians, wanted always to appear to "have it all together," despite their crumbling on the inside, the younger generations are coming forward and talking about their struggles and seeking solutions, and that is a good thing.

As to the perceived stigma of seeking help for a mental or emotional health issue, no one—and I mean no one—"has it all together" for the entirety of their lives. I am not writing of living a sin-free, perfect life, for we know there is only one who can claim that mantle. I am talking about living a human life fully balanced with Christ-like mental and emotional health. We're all in a state of brokenness; we all need help and direction along the path of healing.

I would suggest that all people, at some point in their life, will deal with a crisis involving their emotions or thought processes. It may be chronic abuse of a substance; it may be grief that never subsides; or it might be anger, stress, or fear that permeates their lives and affects their relationship with the Lord and with others. I can guarantee you know or love someone who is struggling with these issues right now or will do so in the near future.

Unfortunately, churches have so often neglected these issues in people's lives. Churches have failed in helping the people who need help the most, due to the false belief that a Christian will not or should not struggle with these issues. Because of this false idea, many in the church feel shame; many stigmatize those who are suffering; and unfortunately, many pastors don't see the need to confront these issues head-on. As a result, people often attend the church and receive no help, or they leave the church to seek help from the world. And that is an indictment of all of us who call ourselves by His name. God has given us a responsibility as His church to minister His love and His grace with hurting, broken people.

Jesus, at His first message at the synagogue in Nazareth, opened the Scriptures to Isaiah the prophet and said, "The Lord has anointed Me to preach." He then spoke of preaching to the poor and healing the blind. And He also declared that He came "to set the captive free." In other words, to deliver people who were bound by the chains of their emotions, feelings, addictions, fears, stresses, shame, and unhappiness.

Perhaps you're thinking, "Well, I'm a Christian. I shouldn't suffer from depression, grieve to this extent, or be a slave to this drink, this lust, or this unhealthy emotion." That is false thinking.

We are all born in a broken condition. We have all fallen into sin. We are all birthed with a bent. Our minds are fallen; our lives are fallen before God. And it is only until we are redeemed that we can begin to really heal and find hope again.

When we come to faith in Jesus Christ, we still have problems and pain from our past, but we are redeemed. And once redeemed, we can then be restored and start truly recovering. But this is a lifelong experience, as we continue to grow in our Christlikeness.

In 1 Thessalonians 5:23, we're told: *"Now may the God of peace himself sanctify you completely, and may your whole spirit and soul and body be kept blameless at the coming of our Lord Jesus Christ."*

Note those three words: spirit, soul, and body. Churches tends to focus on the spirit, sometimes to the neglect of addressing the issues of the body and the soul.

In fact, many don't know the difference between the spirit and the soul. The difference is very small, but very important. In fact, the writer of Hebrews tells us that it takes the sword of the Spirit, the Word of God, to divide the soul and the spirit. The spirit is the part of you that is made for God. It's the spiritual life. It's the part of you that will live forever! The soul is the inner you ... the mind, the emotions, the intellect, and the will.

Now if you are not a believer and follower of Jesus, then your spirit is not alive; it is dead. Your spirit is regenerated ... born again ... when you come alive in Christ. But Jesus died not only for your sins, but for your shame, pain, and hurt. He died to save your spirit, but He rose again so that He could exemplify the perfect soul.

The Scripture says, *"Have this mind among yourselves, which is yours in Christ Jesus"* (Philippians 2:5). In other words, because of Christ's being alive in you, start thinking and acting like Jesus. If you think like Christ, the negativity, fears, shame, and unhealthy desires and reactions can be defeated. Begin by contemplating the greatness and the goodness of God. Receive the mind of Christ. His presence is in all who believe.

Did you know that words such as *happiness, joy, blessedness, favor, merriment,* and *gladness* are used more than 2,500 times in the Bible? Why? Because as Jesus said, *"I came that they may have life and have it abundantly"* (John 10:10).

God wants you to be happy and your soul healthy. God has promised each of us that we can find wholeness and completeness in Him. Our faith, coupled with His abundant, overflowing grace, brings salvation. Our daily seeking to be different from the world—so filled with anger, fear, depression, and substances, and consumed with the flesh—and seeking to be Christlike in all our affairs is the process of sanctification. It is a lifelong process and struggle, but it is the only path to true wholeness, to true mental and emotion health.

We should rest and find peace in our spirit's salvation but work with steadfastness toward the healing of our soul. In order to do so, we must know the mentality of Christ and dedicate and discipline ourselves to seek it every day, all day, in all our affairs.

First, make a decision in your life that you will seek those things which are above, so that you can hear His voice and know His spirit. Isaiah 26:3 says, *"You keep him in perfect peace whose mind is stayed on you, because he trusts in you."*

If you want your mind to recover from the past and the baggage and the brokenness that you bring even into a relationship with God and others, then you must make a decision to possess the mind of Christ.

Second, you must discipline yourself to practice the mind of Christ. Just as you can train and reshape your body, you can train your brain to be healthy and whole. We all have undisciplined thinking, cluttered by the noise in our heads. When are we ever still enough to hear ourselves think, much less hear God speak? And so that's why it is vital to your spiritual, emotional and physical health to find rest for your soul. Jesus said, *"Come unto me all you that labor and are heavy laden, and I will give you rest"* (Matthew 11:28). Rest for your soul. Because that's when we hear the still small voice, and we begin disciplining our minds.

Paul said to Timothy, *"... for God gave us a spirit not of fear but of power and love and self-control"* (2 Timothy 1:7). That means a disciplined mind. Eastern religions and their meditations ask their adherents to empty their minds. An impossible task. The Scriptures tell us to mediate and fill our minds with God's Word! We need to nourish our souls daily with God's Word.

I pray that in reading this book, you or someone you love exchanges Satan's lies for God's truth. That you will exchange your anxiety, stress, grief, and fears for God's peace. That you will exchange your sin, shame, and shattered life for His grace and mercy. That you will exchange your loneliness, alienation, and isolation for His presence and His comfort in your life. If you are hurting today, you have found the right book. And I pray that you can find help in Jesus Christ, in His Word, and among God's people.

The intention of this book is to throw a lifeline to anyone

who would take hold. Whether you or a loved one is dealing with the chains of addiction, the pain of loss, or issues with anger, temptation, shame, stress or fear, in these pages I pray you will find hope in Christ and the help and empowerment of the Holy Spirit to break free and begin afresh.

—Jack Graham

chapter one

HELP! I'M AFRAID

The first issue we tackle in this book is fear, because fear is the underlying emotion to all of the other emotions and mental health issues we will discuss in this book. The fear of future results leads us to stress. The fear we will never be with our loved ones again leads us to never-ending, engulfing grief. The fear that events or relationships won't meet our expectations leads us to anger. The fear that we will always be unhappy can pull us into depression. The fear we will always feel alone obviously creates loneliness. The fear that we cannot change something about ourselves or that we are not sufficient leads to shame.

DEFINING FEAR

Fear is a normal part of being human. At its base level, its purpose is to alert us to danger, and it is crucial to our survival. It's a primitive emotion that triggers a fight or flight response and gets us into a highly alert state. Fear is natural.

As we read in Proverbs 9:10, we see that *"The fear of the Lord is the beginning of wisdom...."* Fear is good when it's a healthy respect for something that is bigger than you. But when your fear is focused on things that really have no power over you, then your fear is actually idolatry, because you're ascribing power to something that's powerless. But as believers, we can choose whether we will fear the right things or the wrong things.

People process fear differently. Depending on past experiences and personality types, the trigger from the emotional experience of fear can be positive or negative. It is in the emotional reaction to fear where the problems arise.

For example, some people love to experience the adrenaline from jumping out of a plane. Others could not fathom anything worse!

Fear can prompt some to commit extraordinary acts of courage, and it can paralyze others. Some soldiers charge headlong into an enemy's firing line to save an injured comrade, where others lay cowed at the bottom of their foxhole, despite the pleas and cries of their brothers in arms.

Fear of rejection or a loss of social status can cause some to remain in their addiction, while it can prompt others to cry for help and salvation.

Let me say that fear is a complex issue. There are so many causes, including traumatic experiences and even genetics. But there is one primary reason we are afraid and anxious—we are human. Whether it's post-traumatic stress disorder (PTSD), panic attack, or just common, everyday worry, none of us are exempt. We all need to learn how to control our fears, phobias, and anxieties in Christ—so we're all in on this! And we all need the lessons that follow.

Though 18 percent of people in America suffer from a diagnosed anxiety disorder of some kind, all of us deal with worry on some level. I guarantee, 100 percent of us have dealt with fear at some point in our lives. And unchecked, uncontrolled fears can rob you of your joy and paralyze you from enjoying and experiencing life to the fullest. Fear will literally bury you if you do not get it under control. Fear directly leads to addictions, shame, and never-ending grief; but its two most common side effects are worry and anxiety—in essence *turbo-charged worry*.

A recent study by the World Mental Health Council surveying 14 nations determined that America is the most worried, anxious nation in the world. Fear is as pervasive in our culture as breathing. In this day and age, we are safer and more prosperous than any others in history. Yet, anytime we seem to eradicate one problem, our minds will simply jump to the next one. This is because fear is inevitable.

Our modern society creates extreme psychological pressure. With the world's opinions and expectations readily available on our smartphones and other devices, and frankly, in our faces, it's no wonder there are such extreme divisions and angry people in our society. Add in a secular worldview that is being taught in our public schools and universities and you have the perfect breeding ground for anxiety and fear.

Where there is no God, there is no peace! Where there is no spiritual light, only secularism and narcissism, is there any wonder that many of our young people are asking the question: "Is it worth it to live? How can I keep going on?" And why the suicide rate is astoundingly up among Millennials and Generation Z?

Even those who attend church, love God, and read and study the Bible are not immune, and can struggle with anxieties of all kinds. Just as we can all experience physical pain and disease of the body, we're not immune to emotional and mental anguish. I've never seen so many changes in our churches as we're seeing today. It's clear to me that, as a result, we are experiencing an avalanche of angst and anxiety. People are increasingly burdened and broken, overwhelmed, and over-extended. We are worried, wearied, fearful, and fatigued.

So as we walk through this journey of discovery, let me encourage you not only to be concerned about yourself, but to look out for people all around you who may be battling various kinds of emotional struggles, mental anguish and pain. Let me remind you, we, the Church, are called to *"Bear one another's burdens, and so fulfill the law of Christ"* (Galatians 6:2).

Fear is a huge obstacle to fighting and winning battles. It doesn't make you *fit to fight*. It makes you *fit for failure.* This is why God told Gideon to say to his 32,000 troops, *"Whoever is fearful ... let him return home ..."* (Judges 7:3). Fear is bad for an army; it's infectious and contagious. God wants you to experience victory in your battles, too. Refuse to let fear stand in the way of doing God's will! Your God is the Prince of Peace. So fear not!

John Wayne famously said, "Courage is being scared to death, but saddling up anyway." So let's saddle up, and really deal with the fear and anxiety in our lives.

WHAT DOES THE BIBLE SAY ABOUT FEAR?

I'm told that there are more than 365 "fear-nots" in the Bible—at least one for every day of the year, so that tells me God knows that we are all going to experience fear, anxiety, and worry at some time in our life. And the Bible is filled with examples of men and women who defeated fear, as well as invaluable parables, illustrations, and Scriptures on fear, anxiety, and worry. Let's examine a few so we can learn to defeat fear as God intends us to do.

GOD LOVES US AND DOES NOT WANT US TO LIVE IN FEAR

The more we consider the sovereign love of God, our heavenly Father, the less we will fear!

More than anything, I want you to know that God cares about you. In 3 John 1:2, we see His love and compassion, *"Beloved, I pray that all may go well with you and that you may be in good health, as it goes well with your soul."*

In Matthew 6:25–33, the Sermon on the Mount, Jesus straightforwardly implores us not to fear or worry about anything.

> *"Therefore I tell you, do not be anxious about your life, what you will eat or what you will drink, nor about your body, what you will put on. Is not life more than food, and the body more than clothing? Look at the birds of the air: they neither sow nor reap nor gather into barns, and yet your heavenly Father feeds them. Are you not of more value than they? And which of you by being anxious can add a single hour to his span of life? And why are*

you anxious about clothing? Consider the lilies of the field, how they grow: they neither toil nor spin, yet I tell you, even Solomon in all his glory was not arrayed like one of these. But if God so clothes the grass of the field, which today is alive and tomorrow is thrown into the oven, will he not much more clothe you, O you of little faith? Therefore do not be anxious, saying, 'What shall we eat?' or 'What shall we drink?' or 'What shall we wear?' For the Gentiles seek after all these things, and your heavenly Father knows that you need them all. But seek first the kingdom of God and his righteousness, and all these things will be added to you."

All these things—*everything you need in life*—will be added to you.

So this is Jesus' Word on fear, worry, and anxiety. He's telling us that worry is so unnecessary. It doesn't accomplish or change anything! It's just unhealthy and unproductive, so why allow it to overtake our minds? It's even unholy because it represents a lack of faith.

I can just imagine Jesus—a smile creasing His sun-encrusted face, looking up and seeing birds flying, perhaps even singing, and saying, *"Look at the birds. They don't worry, they don't fret. God just takes care of them."* Jesus even said in

Matthew 10:29 that not one sparrow will fall to the ground without God's knowing and caring about that one little bird. And if God takes care of the birds, don't you know He will take care of you, believers? He promised!

He also told us to *"look at the fields"*—look at nature. Often when we are stressed or feeling anxious and pressured, one of the best things we can do is just get away. Even if it's in your own backyard, find a place where you can look at the trees, hear the birds, notice the flowers, soak in God's creation, and find peace in that. Marvel and find peace in what God has made—an ocean, a mountain, a rose, the face of a small child—and take a deep breath. God made it all, and He made you, and He cares about you more than you could ever imagine.

I am reminded of 1 John 4:18, *"There is no fear in love, but perfect love casts out fear. For fear has to do with punishment, and whoever fears has not been perfected in love."* I like the way the New Living Translation says it: *"Such love has no fear, because perfect love expels all fear."* Now, I don't love perfectly, but God does! And if I believe that God truly loves me and wants the best for my life, it is His perfect love, the perfect love of the Father for you and me, that expels fear and anxiety. We just need to let that penetrate our mind and heart.

Philippians 4:19 says, *"And my God will supply every need*

of yours according to his riches in glory in Christ Jesus." So God provides for our every need, physically, financially, emotionally. But remember, He knows our needs and wants, but fulfills our needs. All those things that you're worried about, God said, "I will take care of this. Trust Me. Worship Me. Pray."

God's peace is something you can't get in a pill; you can't get it in another person; and you can't get it in pie (as much as I love pie)! It's something that truly only God gives. *"Fear not, for I am with you; be not dismayed, for I am your God; I will strengthen you, I will help you, I will uphold you with my righteous right hand"* (Isaiah 41:10).

The bottom line is this: Jesus Christ is Lord! When He is Lord of your life, He is Lord over every circumstance and every situation of your life. The world can offer no greater solution, no healing or antidote to anxiety greater than the presence and the power and the peace of God.

WE HAVE NOTHING TO FEAR

It's been said that 70 percent of all anxiety can be affected positively by changing our thinking. The power of positive thinking is scripturally based: *"For as he thinks in his heart, so is he"* (Proverbs 23:7, NKJV).

Our dear friend, the late Zig Ziglar gave us this well-known acrostic for fear: F-E-A-R: <u>F</u>alse <u>E</u>vidence <u>A</u>ppearing <u>R</u>eal.

You see, fear, anxiety, and worry are just results of listening to the lies of the Enemy. And Satan is a really good liar! Instead, when our focus is on the Word of God and on His promises to take care of us, we begin to hear those lies for what they are—a bluff—and we begin to get smarter.

The word "worry" comes from the old Anglo-Saxon word *würgen* which means to "strangulate." It paints a picture of a wolf at the throat of its prey and it is described as emotional strangulation. In other words, worry, anxiety, and fears of all types will strangle you and choke the life out of you!

And here's my word on worry: Worry and anxiety caused by fear assume responsibility that God never intended for us to have.

God doesn't want us to live in fear because He knows it can hinder us from His work. In 2 Timothy 1:7 we are promised that *"God gave us a spirit not of fear, but of power...."* What this means for you is that feelings of fear aren't from God, they're from Satan; which means as a believer, you can defeat fear! One of the strongest drives for us as humans is the drive for self-preservation. Even Job 2:4 says, *"... All that a man has he will give for his life."* Since this is the case, it only makes sense that one of the strongest human fears is the fear of death. Remember the story of Nehemiah and his fellow wall builders in Jerusalem? They were being threatened with death by a "devil in a prophet's suit" who came to Nehemiah in 6:10–14. This "devil" tried to scare Nehemiah into quitting his God-given task to rebuild the wall of Jerusalem, disobeying God with this lie: "They are coming to kill you by night." But Nehemiah knew this wasn't a message from God because it was a message of fear. So Nehemiah challenged his people, *"Do not be afraid of them. Remember the Lord, who is great and awesome...."* (Nehemiah 4:14).

Perhaps you're being tempted to run away and hide today. Maybe you're ready to quit your job, ditch your church, or even bail out on your marriage and family. But don't run! That message of fear is not from God! His Word to you today is "Fear not."

So much of what we fear, we have no reason to fear. When the disciples of Jesus thought their boat was about to capsize on the Sea of Galilee during the storm, they looked out and they thought they saw a ghost. Needless to say, they had many reasons to be afraid. But what they saw was Jesus—God in the midst of the storm!

But when the disciples saw Him walking on the sea, they were terrified, and said, *"It is a ghost!"* And they cried out in fear. But immediately, Jesus spoke to them, saying: *"Take heart; it is I. Do not be afraid"* (Matthew 14:26–27).

Many times in our lives, the very things we fear are acts of God Himself. These are things that perhaps God has brought into our lives so that we can run to Him ... to find our strength in Him, relish His love, and experience His awesome grace.

Whatever storm you're facing today that's causing you fear, you will find Jesus at the center, beckoning you to follow after Him. Don't be afraid. Trust in God's goodness and love to always bring you back to Him! So it seems the therapy we need ultimately is truth therapy—the truth of God's Word. You see, if we allow it to renew our mind, the Word of God will shape our thinking, and our thoughts will become healthy thoughts. When you're feeling afraid, remember the Lord. Remember His faithfulness. Remember His goodness. Remember that He's your shield and protector. Remember today that the God we serve is great and awesome, and He will not let you down!

THE SOLUTION TO FEAR

We all love the story of David—the lowly teenage shepherd, who facing a violent death, challenged the great warrior giant, Goliath, and in defeating him, won a battle for the Hebrews.

When David first arrived at the battlefield, carrying food for his brothers from home, he was shocked at what he found. He never could have imagined the enormous fear that he saw in the hearts of the armies of Israel.

You see, Goliath's brashness and mockery had completely demoralized the men. But seeing the fear in his countrymen ignited the heart of the champion within David. Look at what he said to King Saul, *"Let no man's heart fail because of him. Your servant will go and fight with this Philistine"* (1 Samuel 17:32).

Now pay attention to what happens next. After seeing David's determination, his own brothers and even the king tried to discourage him from fighting Goliath, fearing for his life. And they tried to equip him, in a physical sense, to fight like a soldier. But this would have been an enormous mistake, and David knew it. David knew that the real source of strength ... his authority to fight and defeat the giant ... was in God. And this same authority has been given to you, too! Sometimes people will try to discourage you, too. But be like David, full of the determination that comes from knowing the greatness of your God!

I've read David's story and preached about it for many, many years, but it wasn't until recently that I honed in on a little phrase in the story. It says when the moment came—when it was time, when it was go time—he ran to the battle. He actually ran straight at the giant! And proclaimed *"This day the Lord will deliver you into my hand.... For the battle is the Lord'S, and he will give you into our hand"* (1 Samuel 17:46–47). I want you to let these words that David spoke to Goliath take root in your heart. They reveal the source of David's authority and the key to his victory.

David ran headlong to confront his fears with Goliath, and in the power of the name of God, Goliath fell! But some years later, pursued by Saul, fearing for his life, and perhaps starving in the Judean wilderness, David still had no fears and penned the most often quoted and most comforting verse on fear, Psalm 23:4: *"Even though I walk through the valley of the shadow of death, I will fear no evil, for you are with me; your rod and your staff, they comfort me."* David knew that regardless of his dire circumstances, the Good Shepherd who cared for him was with him, and in that protection, he could rest.

Is there a menacing shadow looming over your life—a giant-sized challenge or problem that taunts you and keeps you from living a victorious life in Christ Jesus? Well, if there is, don't give up! You and I are going to take a lesson from young David, the giant-slayer, and discover a vital key to defeating the giants in our paths. And the giant of fear in your life will fall when you run to the battle in the power of God, in the name of Jesus. Whether you are facing an enormous personal crisis, a financial disaster, or some other type of hideous giant, there's something I want you to do. Say these words with me right now, "The battle is the Lord's!" Say it again, "The battle is the Lord's!"

He made it very clear to us that we don't need to be consumed with worry, and in John 14:27, Jesus even gave us His peace when He was near to facing the most fearful event imaginable—the Cross.

> *"Peace I leave with you; my peace I give to you. Not as the world gives do I give to you. Let not your hearts be troubled, neither let them be afraid."*

We must build our lives on the sure foundation of the Word of God. I can't emphasize this enough. It is absolutely essential for controlling our minds and maintaining our mental health, so that when the storms of tribulation, trauma, tests, trials and tragedies come our way, we will not be blown away! And Jesus did warn us in John 16:33: *"... In the world you will have tribulation...."*

We can be strong and steady in the storms of life. We can face the gale-force winds that come against us. Because while we face our fears and deal with them every day, we must never become obsessed with them. As I said earlier, 2 Timothy 1:7 says, *"For God has not given us a spirit of fear,"* (that means an obsession with fear) *"but of power and of love and of a sound mind"* (NKJV).

Few emotions are as powerful as fear. It can cause us to do things we wouldn't do under normal circumstances, and it can keep us from doing things we ought to do. When it comes to responding to fear, you can either *react* or you can *act*. Reaction can lead to bad decisions, while Spirit-led action will guide you down the right path. So don't just react to fear, follow the Spirit and act in a constructive, God-honoring way.

For some, fear, worry, and anxiety can become an obsession, a stronghold. But two words are the antidote for anxiety of every kind, the complete prescription for peace in our lives. Just two words—*grateful prayer*. That means we pray knowing God will answer us; He will take care of us. When we call on the name of God, we transfer our trust from ourselves to Christ, and receive abundant peace for our panic, pressures, and problems.

Philippians 4:6–7 is the courage we need to sustain us in every trial. You see, God has promised peace beyond our comprehension; and here, He shows us how to live that out.

> *"Do not be anxious about anything, but in everything by prayer and supplication with thanksgiving let your*

requests be made known to God. And the peace of God, which surpasses all understanding, will guard your hearts and your minds in Christ Jesus."

He describes it in verse 7 as the peace that surpasses all understanding. So that means we can have peace when it doesn't make sense that we should have peace. Peace that defies our natural understanding. Peace in the storm. Just as in Mark 4, when Jesus was asleep in the boat and the disciples were in fear that their small ship would sink; of course, it didn't. We can be at peace and at rest even when it seems as if our world is about to capsize!

In John 14:27, Jesus said, *"My peace I give to you."* So how does He give it? He gives the answer in Matthew 7:7 where He says, *"Ask, and it will be given to you; seek, and you will find; knock, and it will be opened to you."* So, when you find yourself strangled by worry, pray and practice His presence. Pray and unleash His grace and mercy to attack and defeat anxiety. Pray and watch God work!

FINAL THOUGHTS ON FEAR

As Christians, we accept Christ as our personal Savior. We accept His will; we accept His laws, and we're also asked in the Bible to accept the trials that come our way, accept them fully, and accept the perseverance that they produce in us.

But that's exactly the opposite of what an anxiety sufferer wants to do—you want to fight it as much as you can, tooth and nail, and try to get out of it. Or just stay at home, stay in bed, and wish it away. It's so easy to dwell on the feelings that you have, and that's the worst way because it's like adding fuel to the fire.

When something is wrong with me, with our family, or with the church, I immediately think I have to fix it first. I think, if I don't worry, if I don't get in the middle of this and fix it, then bad things are going to happen! But it's the opposite! If I would give it to God first, He could take care of it before I got my hands all over it!

Cast all your anxieties on Him, because He cares for you (1 Peter 5:7). When we cast our fears on Him, and truly give them to Him, He can take care of them. But He can't if we keep hanging on to those fears. This is where we exercise our faith to just let go. You really can trust God with anything and everything that concerns you.

2 Timothy 1:12 says, *"... But I am not ashamed, for I know whom I have believed, and I am convinced that he is able to guard until that day what has been entrusted to me."*

God is saying to us, "Give it to Me. Entrust it to Me." He is able to guard what you give Him.

We are healed of our anxious fears when we give them to Jehovah Yahweh Shalom, the God of peace. He's our Lord Jesus Christ who promised us this peace. He is the Great Physician and He is the Prince of Peace. So pray and turn your worries to grateful prayer.

chapter two

HELP! I'M STRESSED

Baseball and apple pie once represented all that was good about the American way of life. Now, baseball is interrupted by mobile phones and apple pie comes from the microwave and hardly has time to fill the house with aromatherapy.

The pace of life for most Americans has taken on a survivalist mentality. A recent survey revealed that 89 percent of Americans reported they experience high levels of stress everyday. Nearly 90 percent! That's almost all of us.

Not surprisingly, the stress-laden era in which we live has been referred to as the "Age of Anxiety." There is pressure on business owners to stay competitive in the marketplace. There is pressure on workers to hold down a job. There is pressure on moms and dads to raise responsible kids. There is pressure on those kids to juggle increasingly busy lives. Most people are stretched now more than ever.

JACK GRAHAM

When I was a child, my mother frequently prepared meals using a pressure cooker. Every now and then, I would come in from playing outside to find that silver pot starting to shake, rattle, and roll. The hint of a whistle would grow into a scream as the pressure mounted inside; and before you knew it, our kitchen ceiling was dripping with potatoes and green beans.

I've never forgotten that pressure cooker. In fact, there have been seasons of my adult life when I have become that pressure cooker. A melodious whistle would wind up becoming a scream as the pressure inside of me mounted, and ultimately, my top would blow.

Perhaps you can relate.

Maybe you know what it's like to be a living, breathing pressure cooker, the type of person who is maxed out, burned out, and ready to explode. The demands on your life—those things that you want to do, need to do, can and must do overwhelm the amount of time that you have to do them; and the end result is a great deal of stress. It's not a fun place to be.

The bad news is far too many Christ-followers have chosen this way of life. The good news is that another option exists. We can stay inside our stress, or we can move to a place of peace.

As a pastor, I feel compelled to address the spiritual dimension of stress and help you find a biblical response to the pace of life we keep. There are thousands of guides out there claiming to have the cure for stress. Websites, books, apps, and podcasts will promise foolproof results for the severely stressed out.

If you've tried the remedies and failed, I have some hope and encouragement for you that doesn't need a money-back guarantee. I promise you the Good Shepherd will listen and bring you to a place of peace. Remember, He knows you better than anyone.

THE EFFECTS OF STRESS

Stress has infiltrated our homes, our schools, our jobs, our minds, and our relationships. Stress attacks, debilitates, and destroys us physically, emotionally, mentally, and spiritually.

You and I both have heard the reports of what stress and worry and pressure can do to us physically—fatigue, headache, insomnia, sore or achy muscles, heart palpitations, frequent colds, chest pain, abdominal cramps, nausea, not to mention the major coronary issues it causes. Stress has been linked to all the leading causes of death, including heart disease, cancer, lung ailments, accidents, addiction, and suicide.

We certainly know what it can do to us emotionally and mentally—who doesn't know someone on anti-depressants these days? The emotional signs of stress include: anxiety, nervousness, depression, anger, frustration, worry, fear, irritability, impatience, and short temper. Nearly half of all American workers suffer from symptoms of burnout, a disabling mental and emotional reaction to stress on the job.

And then there are spiritual ramifications as the pressure inside of us builds. The Bible is filled with occurrences of patriarchs, prophets, and disciples succumbing to the pressures of stress. Moses disobeying God by striking the rock in anger. Elijah running from Ahab and Jezebel. Peter denying Christ three times. All sins of anger, disobedience, and fear caused by stress that negatively affected their faith. Therefore, do not lose heart, be encouraged, for even the mighty heroes of the faith struggled.

THE ORIGINS OF STRESS

But where does the pressure come from? And why do we take it so hard? In my experience I've seen at least five origins of stress. See which, if any, apply to you.

The first origin of stress is *temperament*. Some people are wired to be pressure cookers. If life doesn't present a dramatic situation, they'll go create one on their own. They thrive on stress—or so they think—and expect others to do the same.

A second origin of stress is what I call the desire to acquire. You would think that wealth, riches, and success would provide more security and greater serenity in life. But in fact, the opposite is true. If your possessions get a grip on you, anxiety surely will follow. As Ecclesiastes 5:12 says, *"the full stomach of the rich will not let him sleep."* Frankly, I'd rather be poor and well rested!

And then there's media hype. Our grandparents never saw the effects of crime in the streets six states over and wars exploding around the world. But with news at our thumbs 24 hours a day, we can be as informed as we so desire. The end result of all that information is more than a well-informed mind; it's also a well-stressed life.

A fourth cause of stress is simply our life experiences. None of us were born worriers. Worry is a learned behavior, and the way we learn it is via our experiences in life. People lose their loved ones. They lose their health. They lose their jobs. They lose financial security. The pressures mount and the stresses take their toll, and worry becomes our constant state. Sadly, I know too many believers today who bear the wild eyes of an animal being cut off from its source of air. There is panic. There is fear. There is a perpetual sense of worry. This is not the life of abundance God promised.

There is a fifth origin I've noticed, and that is the pace of life. We pile too much onto each day, we rarely take time to relax, and then we wonder why we feel so tense. We have no down time. We have 16 minutes to eat dinner before heading to the next practice, meeting, or event, and fall into bed exhausted and unfulfilled.

THE SOLUTION TO STRESS

We all know that stress is a relentless enemy. But we fight to the point of exhaustion, trying to keep up, always losing small battles along the way in the form of tension and pressure. If all of this sounds too familiar, then I have good news for you.

What amazing promises! Whether you are winning or losing your war against stress, you will find inspiring hope and practical guidance in the Word and particularly God's plan for internal peace.

The plan for lasting stress relief is Psalm 23. Aside from a recipe for dealing with stress and finding peace, it is a compelling picture of what the place called "peace" is all about. We know a peaceful existence is possible; we're just not all that good at living it out.

> *The LORD is my shepherd; I shall not want.*
> *He makes me lie down in green pastures.*

> *He leads me beside still waters.*
> *He restores my soul.*
> *He leads me in the paths of righteousness*
> *for his name's sake.*
> *—Psalm 23:1–3*

If you know and follow the Good Shepherd, the Lord Jesus Christ, you can be sure that you are not fighting a losing battle.

If you're ready to stop the madness and breathe, to arrest your worry and find peace, to halt your pace and pause, your God is ready to guide you. Remember, *"God will supply every need of yours according to his riches in glory in Christ Jesus"* (Philippians 4:19).

When life's storms gather above us and when turbulent waters rise, we can rest in the knowledge that our Good Shepherd is working diligently to seek out a silent, still stream.

In the poetic verses of Psalm 23, you and I are promised a destination marked by rest, refreshment, and restoration. And personally, I could use a dose of all three.

FINDING REST

I look back on my most recent series of "pressure cooker" days and realize it's no accident that the verse says God "makes" His people lie down in those green pastures He graciously provides. The psalmist doesn't say that God "invites" us or that He "encourages" us to lie down. It says quite specifically that we must be made to stop and rest.

Sometimes God has to put us flat on our backs in order to get us to suspend our busyness and be still. He's done it in my life, and likely He's done it in yours, too.

Why do most of us find it so hard to stop and rest? Why does our Shepherd have to make us lie down? I think it's because we have convinced ourselves that we aren't accomplishing anything unless we're busy, unless we're running in several directions at once. If we stop and rest, someone else may catch up and pass us. But have you ever noticed that it's the pauses in life that refresh us?

Appropriate pauses, necessary breaks, a chance to stop and breathe—whose life wouldn't wind up better with a little more of these things?

A life without rest, an existence in which we never pause to commune with our Shepherd or find out what He expects of us, is not life as God intended it to be.

I'd like to share two practices I adopted many years ago that help me train my focus on God during my periods of peace. Consider them my gift to you, from one pressure cooker to another.

The first is to meditate on God's Word. The psalmist advised us to meditate day and night upon the Word of God (Psalm 1:2). Later he reminds us we will find strength from His Word. *"Let the words of my mouth and the meditation of my heart be acceptable in your sight, O LORD, my rock and my redeemer"* (Psalm 19:14). We must take time to hear from God, to listen to God, to meditate upon the Word of God, then we will find strength.

It is especially critical for people like us, who thrive on constant activity and growth, to power off all devices every once in a while and take time to hear from God. God is more interested in our spiritual growth and strength than He is in our frantic activity. He knows that we will be right back to our completely stressed existences if we don't take our times of rest with Him seriously.

As we sit down to rest and focus our hearts on God and on His Word, He can speak to us. Remember, God doesn't speak in the thunder or in the lightning, God speaks in the still, small voice of His Spirit as He engages us with His Word.

The second way to pause is based on a powerful verse in Isaiah 30:15, which says, *"... in quietness and in trust shall be your strength."* Interestingly, it is possible, probable even, for us to grow stronger when we're doing nothing but waiting on God.

Our gracious Good Shepherd has designed a system whereby we can find true rest only in Him. And it is when we choose to "be still and know" that He is God that we see our shoulders loosen, our heart rate normalize, our lives become sane once more. When we believe God for true rest, we allow our existence to untangle, our emotions to breathe, and our ever-pressured schedules to relax.

FINDING REFRESHMENT

Not only does our Good Shepherd provide rest, but according to the end of Psalm 23:2, He also provides refreshment.

"He leads me beside still waters," the verse promises, which is important when you consider how sheep feel about still waters. Being the easily disturbed creatures that they are, sheep will not drink beside a raging, rushing river. They are too afraid they might fall in, and who wouldn't be challenged by the prospect of swimming in a wooly overcoat?

So, in deference to the sheep's desires on this front, their good shepherd will hunt high and low for a silent, still stream. If he can't find one, he will dip the crook of his staff into the rough water and move stones around until he forms a little dam where still waters can form. He is that committed to his sheeps' refreshment; he is that committed to their care.

No matter what we accomplish or acquire in this life—if we neglect or ignore our spiritual life, we will never feel truly satisfied.

Do you need a calming, cooling, refreshing drink of water right now? Perhaps the stream of your life is rushing by with such speed and turbulence that you cannot find "still waters" from which to drink. Seek Him and you will find rest and refreshment beyond explanation.

The God who created us knows exactly what we need. Allow God to speak to you and guide you as you rearrange the stones in your stream and provide a still place for your spirit.

I love Jesus' promise in John 10:10, which says that Christ came that we might have abundant life, a life overflowing with goodness. This is our Good Shepherd's desire for us, but for us to enjoy it, we first must be clear on what this "abundance" really means.

Matthew 5:6 says, *"Blessed are those who hunger and thirst for righteousness, for they shall be satisfied."* So many people are unsatisfied today because they are hungering and thirsting for happiness instead of righteousness. But God doesn't say that temporal happiness will satisfy our hearts and souls. He says that only righteousness will do the trick. And it is along the path of righteousness, Psalm 23:3 says, that our God indeed will lead us.

Your life can be lived, revitalized, and refreshed. Your God will satiate your hunger and quench your thirst, if only you'll seek the abundance that He alone can provide.

FINDING RESTORATION

There's a final promise that awaits us at the place of peace; He also provides restoration for anyone who seeks it.

In Psalm 23, Jesus Christ is portrayed as a shepherd, one who is wholly devoted to the care of His sheep. And if there is one thing that sheep need, it's a dose of devoted care. Sheep are dirty and dumb, but more significant than that, they are easily distracted.

The Good Shephard has an incredible propensity to rescue the ones He loves. After all, it's one thing to lay down our burdens, but quite another to be offered a loving hand back up.

There are times when a sheep will become "cast down" because the poor animal has fallen into a crevice or has tripped into a hole. Either way, once a sheep is down, he will flail about on his back with all four feet standing straight in the air and have no way whatsoever to get up. He just doesn't have the dexterity to rise from that pit. He's down and out, and the only thing that will deliver him is for the shepherd to happen by.

Four times in Psalm 42 and 43, the psalmist David referred to his soul as "downcast." Surely you can relate to his plight. At one time or another, you and I both have known what it is to have a downcast soul. Our spirits are low; our efforts feel futile, and we can't seem to stand ourselves up. It's at this moment that our Good Shepherd happens by. He gently picks us up. He graciously restores our souls.

Too many people believe that God is somehow out to get them, but this line of thinking could not be further from the truth. God loves you and His purpose is to restore you. I relish what Joel 2:25 says along these lines: *"I will restore to you the years that the swarming locust has eaten...."* Our very good God will restore even the years that found us wandering away, and He will return us to fellowship with Him.

What a wonderful Savior is Jesus, our Lord—our Restorer and Rescuer, too. For our weariness, He provides green pastures; for our worries, He gives us still waters; and for our wanderings, He restores us as only our Good Shepherd can do. These are the promises that await us, my friend, when we willingly choose to seek His place of peace.

If there is one person in Scripture who proves we not only can cope with stress but conquer it as well, it is surely the Apostle Paul. More than any other, Paul shows us what it looks like for the promises of peace to play out in the life of a believer.

Paul (having been beaten, exiled, tortured, shipwrecked, starved, and imprisoned) knew something about stress, and here is his wisdom:

> *Rejoice in the Lord always: again 1 will say, Rejoice. Let your reasonableness be known to everyone. The Lord is at hand; do not be anxious about anything, but in everything by prayer and supplication with thanksgiving let your requests be made known to God. And the peace of God, which surpasses all understanding, will guard your hearts and your minds in Christ Jesus.* Philippians 4:4–7

As I look at Paul's words, I am reminded of the three practices that led him perpetually to the place called peace.

PAUSING TO PRAY

Before Paul indulged his anxieties and concerns, he invited God's presence through prayer.

"*Do not be anxious about anything,*" Paul wrote in Philippians 4:6, "but in everything by prayer and supplication with thanksgiving Iet your requests be made known to God."

In this life, we have a choice, which is either to fret or to pray. We can carry our concerns and try to fix them ourselves, or we can cast them at the foot of the Cross, fully confident that God knows, He sees, and He cares about our troubles and fears. Paul had every reason to fret, and yet he chose first to pray. I think there's a lesson here for us both.

PAUSING TO PRAISE

Not only did Paul pray, but he prayed, according to verse 6, rejoicingly with thanksgiving or praise. There is a beautiful old song that encourages this very behavior:

> *Turn your eyes upon Jesus*
> *Look full in his wonderful face,*
> *And the things of earth will grow strangely dim*
> *In the light of his glory and grace*

When it seems the "things of earth" are overtaking the landscape of your life, look full into the wonderful face of your Good Shepherd and simply say, "Thanks." Find something to thank Him for, and see if your troubles, like Paul's, don't grow strangely dim as well.

PAUSING TO GAIN PERSPECTIVE

There was a third practice that enabled Paul to experience

the true rest that God alone provides, and it's found in Philippians 4:8–9:

> *Finally, brothers, whatever is true, whatever is honorable, whatever is just, whatever is pure, whatever is lovely, whatever is commendable, if there is any excellence, if there is anything worthy of praise, think about these things. What you have learned and received and heard and seen in me—practice these things, and the God of peace will be with you.*

Paul understood that our character is the sum total of our thoughts. If we think healthy thoughts and holy thoughts, we'll become healthy and holy. If our thoughts are constantly pessimistic and sinful, we'll become the worst version of ourselves in a flash. So, if you wish to get rid of worrisome thoughts that can plague a divided mind, then fill up your heart with the living Word of God. Those things which are good and holy and wholesome. Paul says to treasure up these things.

You may say, "Well, I can't help what I think. I have all these problems in the past, all these pressures today, and I just feel completely overwhelmed." If that's you, I challenge you to take a timeout and get still before God.

God has so constructed us and created us that we can only think one thought at a time. And if I'm thinking what is right, I can't be thinking what is not right. If I am thinking what is good, I can't be thinking what is not good. If I'm thinking what is positive and uplifting and praiseworthy, then I cannot be thinking that which is damaging, detrimental, and driving me downward.

When I feel myself fretting and becoming fearful, I quote a Scripture silently in my mind. Often this occurs at night, and I notice that as I mull over the inspired Word of God, I am able to pillow my head on His promises and sleep like a baby all night. I am able to awaken in the morning with my thoughts focused on Him and my heart ready to worship Him one more day. What a priceless gift straight from God, this ability to train our thoughts!

Several years ago, my doctor ordered me to take a stress test. Electrodes were attached to my chest and arms while a big machine was rolled into position, and once everything was set, I was asked to run on a treadmill for a while. A long while, if you ask me.

Fortunately, I made it through the test without passing out, but the experience still left its mark. I discovered that no matter how hard or fast my weary legs ran in their futile attempt to keep up, to avoid falling behind, to maintain the frenzied pace, I just couldn't keep going forever. Eventually I had to stop.

Life works like that, too.

In the same way that I had to stop running before my doctor could assess my condition and offer solutions for what ailed me, you and I have to halt our reckless pace in order for God to intervene. And I'm talking about a shift that's more than superficial here. Sure, we can appear peaceful and tranquil and still. We can paste a smile on our face, steady our gaze, and pray that our harried, hurried, and hassled state doesn't betray us to everyone we know. But the One who first loved us, who created us, who longs to set our lives aright sees through. "If you will earnestly slow down and seek me," He offers, "I'll lead you to a brand new place—a peaceful place."

I want to draw your attention to the fact that it was only when Paul was willing to pause that he experienced the full peace of God, the full power of God. Through his prayers, his praise, and his regained perspective, he was able to have his heart and mind guarded by the *"peace of God"* as verse seven says, *"which surpasses all understanding."*

I've seen this dynamic firsthand. It would be impossible for me to count the number of times that I have been by the side of pain-wrought people who were facing the most indescribable of situations with a family member in an ICU or steps from a close friend's graveside. Despite the suffering and the tears, there is incredible peace. It's the peace that passes understanding, and if you are walking in an intimate relationship with Jesus Christ today, you know exactly what I'm talking about. There is serenity and security to be found in Christ that is available nowhere else in the world. This is the peace that Paul spoke of.

I never advise people to expect the magical disappearance of their problems when they surrender their lives to Christ. It just doesn't work that way. It can't work that way, because peace is not the absence of problems and pressure. Peace is the addition of God's strength to face the storms. This is the hope we can inhabit, each and every day.

A PRAYER FOR PERSONAL PEACE

This day, and when life's stresses seem to overwhelm you, ask God for the ability to exhale all that ails you and to breathe in His righteousness, His peace. Your soul will relish its long-awaited revival, and your body will thank you for the break.

Good Shepherd, I thank You that You lead me and You feed me.

Help me to learn to drink deeply from the still waters.

Lead me to green pastures so I can experience Your rest.

Lord, help me to gain the strength I need to live for You.

Thank You for tracking me down, for seeking me out and bringing me home.

Amen.

chapter three

HELP! I'M ADDICTED

There is a good chance that you or someone close to you—a spouse, a child, a parent, a friend, or a coworker—is struggling with a powerful addiction. If you have an addiction, then you are wrestling with demons that you don't quite understand and feel powerless to control. If you have a loved one suffering from an addiction, then you have witnessed time and time again the seemingly powerlessness to control the habit or behavior, despite knowing the behavior hurts those he or she loves the most.

We know addictions dominate and ultimately destroy lives. Addicted individuals are engaging in self-defeating, self-depreciating, self-destructive behavior that will destroy their physical and spiritual life. Their behavior has become more important than their spouse, friends, and family members. It becomes more important to them than their church and fellow believers. It becomes more important than their career or calling in life. Addiction takes over like chains fashioned from seemingly unbreakable iron.

If you're struggling with sin, addictions, or habits that are holding you back, this chapter is designed with you in mind. Maybe you've tried therapy; you've tried self-help books; you've tried yoga; and you've tried religion. None of that has worked because it's all externally focused.

Now, if you face an addiction or dependency of any kind, I encourage you to seek professional counseling. There are very fine counselors, therapists, and doctors who can assist and help us through the mental and sometimes physical chains of addiction. Certainly, if that professional is a Christian, he or she better understands the spiritual framework of dealing with the psychology of the soul and the mind. Psychology can help us understand what's wrong with us, but only Jesus can break the physical, emotional, and spiritual chains that keep us from living victoriously through Him.

The purpose of this chapter is to show you what God's Word says regarding breaking the chains of addiction in your life. You need to understand what God says about your problem. You need to know the biblical truth because God made you to be free! Jesus can break every chain of addiction, whether it is drugs, alcohol, sexual immorality of any kind, gambling, anger, or bitterness. Jesus can break every chain if you allow yourself to experience His power in your life, if you seek the power of Christ in your life.

Addiction has been defined as "being controlled or consumed with a substance, thought process, emotion, or activity to an unhealthy degree." The reality is that addiction is simply a chain that enslaves us. It is a chain that controls us and keeps us from becoming who God intended us to be. In 2 Peter 2:19, we find a wise warning: *"For whatever overcomes a person, to that he is enslaved."* The addiction may be to a substance, such as alcohol, drugs, prescription medications, tobacco, or food. The addiction may be behavioral, such as gambling, sexual immorality, or even over-work. The addiction may also be to an emotion, such as anger, grief, or negativity. The reality is, all sin is addictive, and can ultimately become habitual.

We are an addicted culture. There is no need to provide statistic after statistic showing that the moral fabric, public health, and financial stability of our society are being ripped apart and degraded by addictive substances and behaviors. How many lives have been taken as a result of alcohol and drug abuse? How many marriages have been destroyed because of a spouse who is unfaithful either in deed or thought? How many people have been made destitute because of a bet on a game of chance or sport? How many families have been hurt or destroyed because the heads of the house cannot seem to put aside work long enough to spend time with those who love them most? The extreme fallout of addiction on spouses, children, family, friends and our society and culture is mortifying. Yet, addictions not only persist, but seem to be increasing in variety and intensity. The types of addictions and the number of people ensnared by them seem to be growing exponentially. The world is developing new substances and technologies which will only swell the ranks of our addicted culture. Satan, of course, rejoices in our fashioning of shackles of sin and dependence to ensnare and trap ourselves.

Did you know the greatest Christian who ever lived, the Apostle Paul, struggled with a spiritual battle and with addictive sin itself? In Romans 7:14–15, Paul wrote, *"For we know that the law is spiritual, but I am of the flesh, sold under sin. For I do not understand my own actions. For I do not do what I want, but I do the very thing that I hate."* In verse 17, he wrote: *"So now it is no longer I who do it, but sin that dwells within me."* Paul went on to write: *"Who will deliver me from this body of death?"* (Romans 7:24). How could the greatest Christian who ever lived have also written, *"For I know that nothing good dwells in me, that is, in my flesh. For I have the desire to do what is right, but not the ability to carry it out"* (Romans 7:18 ESV)? Because addiction and sin were trying to take over the thoughts and actions of perhaps the most devout hero of the faith and the man who had the most remarkable salvation experience ever recorded.

We all know the verse: *"Therefore, if anyone is in Christ, he is a new creation. The old has passed away; behold, the new has come"* (2 Corinthians 5:17). Yet, why do we as believers do those things that we try not to do and don't do the things that we want to do? Because we all have a human heart that is, according to the prophet, *"Despicable and desperately wicked"* (Jeremiah 17:9). Now in Christ we have a new heart and a new life, but here's a truth that you need to grasp. If you are a follower, a believer in the Lord Jesus, you are still in the flesh. You still inhabit this mortal human body in a fallen world, a world that wants to tear you down and enslave you. The Spirit of the Living Christ is now in you, but that doesn't mean that you cease to deal with the flesh and the desires and your own humanity. And in fact, this will be a constant struggle all the days of your life. We all have issues and temptations, propensities in our lives that we deal with daily. Being a Christian does not make you immune to facing and fighting spiritual battles.

Why does Satan bother tempting and lying to believers, knowing that we have been redeemed and will spend eternity with our heavenly Father? Because Satan is the father of lies (John 8:44). Because *"Satan is a thief whose only purpose is to steal, kill and destroy"* (John 10:10). Satan revels in the pain and misery he can cause the children of God. Because Satan wants you to be enslaved to a sin rather than experience the freedom that salvation brings. Because Satan knows a drunken soldier of Christ is a defeated enemy. Because Satan knows a family on the verge of bankruptcy as a result of gambling losses will be torn in two. Because Satan knows the workaholic is not spending the time with his family that they need, nor engaging in good works to further the kingdom. Because addictions not only destroy the life of addicts, but those around them as well. Because as Paul wrote, addictions and sinful thoughts *"led [us] astray from a sincere and pure devotion to Christ"* (2 Corinthians 11:3).

Despite our greater understanding and diagnosis of addictions, and regardless of the innumerable and costly treatments and counseling options for addicts, addictions are still increasing at an exponential rate. The reason is simple: Satan, the father of lies, is still telling us lies, and we still choose to believe those lies. Satan lies to us sinners about that which we are addicted to, and then we lie to ourselves about the nature of our dependence on them.

After 40 years of ministry, I have heard all the excuses and lies. Lies such as "It's just a harmless substance," "Well, I don't really have a problem," "It's not that bad," "It's not that big of a deal," "I can quit any time," "It's not hurting anybody else," "I can't help it; it's just the way I am," or even "God made me this way, and therefore I need this." I keep hearing the same lies from people because Satan keeps repeating the same lies. His method of operation is the same as it was in the Garden of Eden—he lies to us about the true cost and devastating effects of a substance he wants us to ingest or an activity he prods us to engage in.

Recall that in the beautiful paradise of the Garden of Eden, only one rule was commanded by God: Do not eat of the Tree of the Knowledge of Good and Evil. So what did Satan do? Of course, he lied to Adam and Eve to get them to eat the forbidden fruit. Genesis 3 says, "But the serpent said to the woman, "You will not surely die." (Lie! It will kill you ultimately!) "For God knows that when you eat of it your eyes will be opened and you will be like God, knowing good and evil." The first temptation was not to be ungodly; it was to be godly. "You know, God's holding out on you. He doesn't want you to have a pleasurable life; it's OK to eat this fruit."

Satan's primary tool, then and now, is deception. And the same devil, with the same lies that entrapped Adam and Eve in Eden, is attempting to control the way you think. He's trying to get into your head and create a pattern of thinking that, in turn, creates a pattern of behavior that will enslave you. Most people act out their feelings. Their feelings are produced by what they think. So, you start thinking the wrong way, and you start feeling the wrong way, and ultimately, your feelings are acted out in real life. Adam and Eve believed the lies of Satan before they ate of the forbidden fruit. Likewise, people start thinking, and in turn, feeling things such as: "Well, I just don't feel like I love my wife anymore," "I'm unhappy and I need pleasure," or "I'm down; I need something to get me up." And the pattern of thinking and feeling and acting is repeated again and again. Satan has programmed the addict to think his way rather than God's way. When a believer begins to say, "I need this forbidden fruit," that's when Satan is in your head; sin is in your heart; and chains are on your life.

There are two types of addicts, both of whom have bought into Satan's lies: those who do not believe they have an addiction and those who know they are addicted but feel powerless to overcome their dependence.

As to the first—the "deniers"—they have believed the lies so long they don't know the difference between what is true and what is a lie. Well, I've seen it, and you've seen it, too. There are some people who really do not want to get well. They get used to their behavior. They get used to their lives the way they are. So, people often stay addicted to their sin, their pain, their struggle, their stress, their depression, their anger, their anxiety, and their physical-mental addiction, because they refuse to acknowledge the existence of soul-ensnaring addiction in their life. They stay addicted because they're no longer in control of their own life. They are like the person who said, "If I'm lying, and you know that I'm lying, and I know that you know that I'm lying, and you know that I know that you know that I'm lying … isn't that the same as telling the truth?" Some of us have believed the lies of the Enemy so long or the lies we've been telling ourselves so long, that we don't know the difference anymore!

As to the second type of addict—the ones who know they have a problem but feel the chains are unbreakable—they believe they are forever controlled by a substance, a thought process, or an emotion which governs every aspect of their life, including time, money, and energy. These addicts may desperately want to change their behavior patterns, to break the cycle of dependence. However, they believe they are living in inescapable bondage; they cannot break free from their constraints.

These addicts know in their heart of hearts that the substance, emotion or activity they are bound by is not just a sin that damages their marriages, family, career, or finances, but their invaluable eternal soul as well. However, they do not believe healing can occur.

They remind me of the crippled man Jesus met one day at the pool of Bethesda in Jerusalem. As detailed in John 5, there was a belief among the people that when the waters began to stir in this particular pool, it was an angel stirring it. The first one who got in was healed. And so people would go to this pool to be healed. Well, this particular man had been lying at the pool for 38 years! Because he was lame, every time the waters would stir, he would try to get in, but couldn't get there fast enough. And one day Jesus of Nazareth came by and looked at him, and when the man caught His eyes, Jesus said, "Do you want to be made well?" "What! I've been here for 38 years! Why would you ask me, 'Do I want to get well?'" This man was lying there all these years and Jesus wanted him to say, "Yes, I want to get well! Yes, I want to be healed more than anything in my life!" And Jesus healed him. The man had been ill for so long he had given up hope of being healed. This man is like the addict who believes his addiction is an illness which will always afflict him, an unbreakable chain of bondage from which he will never escape. This belief is a lie told by Satan, which, in turn, the addict tells himself. This lie is toxic. This lie minimizes the power of God to remove our shackles and the freedom Christ Jesus brings us through salvation.

So the question remains for both types of addicts, those who deny they have a problem and those who deny they can break free from their addiction: Do you want to be healed?

If you desire to be healed, if you desire to break the chains, then the first thing you need to do is to admit your addiction. It is the first of the 12 steps at Alcoholics Anonymous. Now, interestingly enough, the 12 steps of AA were originally a Christian program to overcome alcohol addictions. The steps have been modified in recent years, but the first of the steps says, "We admitted we are powerless over alcohol—that our lives had become unmanageable." To obtain treatment, healing, and changed lifestyle, the addicted person must confess to God the Father, the Great Physician, that he or she has a problem with a particular substance, behavior, or emotion, before seeking healing for the dependence.

I beg you in the name of Jesus to admit your helplessness. You must deny yourself and trust in the name of Jesus to help stop believing the lies. Admit that you are powerless over pornography, powerless over sensuality, powerless over gambling, powerless to overcome your sin! Confess that you are chained, and say, "I can't live like this anymore! I won't live like this anymore! I refuse to be caught up in the chains of Satan, the chains of my own making!" The way to victory, the way to purity, the way to freedom is to begin by saying "I can't defeat this on my own! I've got a problem! I'm struggling with this. I must now seek the help of God ... the help of Jesus Christ and of His people." Because the good news is, in Christ, we are not powerless!

When you stop believing the lies Satan tells you, the lies your friends tell you, the lies that culture tells you, the lies you tell yourself, and start believing in the truth and Jesus Christ, that's when you'll be free! That's when you'll walk in the Spirit. So no more excuses! Stop believing what Satan says about you and start believing what God says about you! That you are alive in Christ; that you have the power of Christ in you! This is your identity! This is who you are!

Galatians 5:16–24 provides:

> *But I say, walk by the Spirit, and you will not gratify the desires of the flesh. For the desires of the flesh are against the Spirit, and the desires of the Spirit are against the flesh, for these are opposed to each other, to keep you from doing the things you want to do. But if you are led by the Spirit, you are not under the law.*
>
> *Now the works of the flesh are evident: sexual immorality, impurity, sensuality, idolatry, sorcery, enmity, strife, jealousy, fits of anger, rivalries,*

> *dissensions, divisions, envy, drunkenness, orgies, and things like these. I warn you, as I warned you before, that those who do such things will not inherit the kingdom of God. But the fruit of the Spirit is love and joy and peace and patience and kindness, gentleness, faithfulness, self-control; against such things there is no law.*

And those who belong to Christ Jesus have crucified the flesh with its passions and desires.

There's only one thing to do with our flesh and our sinful addictions, and that is to crucify it. You can't modify it, or change it externally. You can decorate it, or make it look better. If you are an alcoholic, then you can't control your consumption of alcohol, regardless of whether you are a homeless person on the street or you're sitting in church wearing a $3,000 suit. Do you desire to be healed? Do you desire to have the shackles of the sinful flesh removed. Do you want your mind purified of the negative things you have thought or your heart as felt?

The way to overcome the desires of the flesh and the addictions of the soul and the body is through the Holy Spirit starving the flesh and feeding the spirit. It's not you just promising to be better or trying harder. If you feed the flesh, guess what happens? You want more and more and more, and you starve the work of the Holy Spirit. But when you feed the Spirit in prayer, in the Word of God, in the praise and the worship of Jesus Christ and in the fellowship of God's people that is genuine, authentic accountability. When you are walking in the Word and walking in the Spirit, then you start winning spiritual battles and peeling back the darkness, not in defeat, but in victory in Jesus Christ! That is a promise!

So I'm telling you, as God's children, you don't have to live the way you're living, but the way to change your behavior is to change what you believe. "You shall know the truth and the truth will set you free!" You have a new name! You have a new nature! You have been born again into the family of God. You are a child of God! You don't live where you used to live! You've moved out! You've moved out of jail and into the liberty and life that is yours in Christ!

So don't say, "Oh, I'm just human, I can't change." That's a lie. That's not who you are. You're better than that. *"You can do all things through Christ who strengthens you"* (Philippians 4:13). Reject the lies of Satan. Quit adding on the chains and the links to the chain. Tear down every idol and watch Jesus cut away the chains. There's a way out. You're no longer enslaved. You're free. And if the Son Jesus will make you free, you will be free indeed.

The Statue of Liberty is a beautiful symbol of freedom. It stands in the New York Harbor and Lady Liberty lifts up a lantern of freedom. She has seven points on her crown inviting, with each of the seven points, the people from the seven seas and the seven continents, to come and find freedom. All of the oppressed and all of the broken and all who are seeking freedom are invited to come to America and find freedom. Emma Lazarus wrote these words that are now inscribed on the Statue of Liberty, inviting "huddled masses yearning to breathe free." God made every person with the desire and the need to be free.

Freedom is not license to do everything you want, but the power to do what you ought. To live in freedom is the promise of God for all. Freedom is such an empowering instinct within the human heart, within the soul of man. No one was made to live in tyranny and bondage, be it to a substance, an emotion, or a habitual desire to sin.

Let freedom reign in your heart because Jesus came to set you free. Jesus said, *"And you will know the truth and the truth will set you free"* (John 8:32). And then He said, *"So if the Son sets you free, you will be free indeed!"* (John 8:36). So the chains that bind us, the habits that hold us back, the sins that enslave us must be broken, and they can be broken in Christ! In Christ you can be set free, and therefore, you are free from the need to pop that pill, or to take that drink, or to look at pornography, or to cheat on your spouse. You're free *not* to buy that lottery ticket or to throw away your income on gambling. You are free to overcome the power of selfish and sinful pleasure.

You may be a Christian struggling with some of these issues, but that is not who you are! You may be *helpless*, but it's not *hopeless!* But you have to be willing to be unchained, to be set free, to be made whole. There's no addiction you can't overcome in the name of Jesus if you understand your true identity. So stop saying to yourself, "I can't win over this sin; I can't defeat this pattern of behavior." You're a new person in Jesus Christ! If you are in Christ, you cannot also say "Oh, I'm just an addict," or "I'm just an adulterer," or "I'm just hooked on tobacco." Quit saying, "My life's never going to get better!" Stop believing the lies that you tell yourself or the lies that the Enemy tells you. That's a lie! If you are in Christ, your life's going to get a whole lot better! Quit saying, "I'm just destined for failure, and I'm just a longtime loser." Stop defining yourself by your behavior, rather than your identity in Christ Jesus. You are not just an addict; rather you are the redeemed and precious child of the Living God, a human who struggles, as the Apostle Paul did, with a thorn in your flesh. You were born to win, to defeat the Enemy! You are alive in Christ, and you can do all things through Christ who strengthens you. You can resist in the name of Jesus the world, the flesh, the devil! In Christ's name, you can break every chain!

We are no longer slaves to sin if we are in Christ! We have been set free. We then need to learn to live in the victory that Christ has given us. Christ is the life-maker and the bondage-breaker! Christ will set us free from sin and its power! Jesus will forgive us and then give us freedom to live in hope and victory every day. You can be free of anything that chains you, anything that controls you, body, mind, soul, and spirit.

chapter four

HELP! I'M LONELY

As we tackle the topic and consider the paralyzing effects of loneliness, we must first ask: What is loneliness?

We all deal with loneliness every day because loneliness is a part of the human condition. It is felt anywhere, anytime, and by anyone. No one is immune and no place is safe.

Consider the different places where you are not alone but still stricken with loneliness. You can be lonely at church. You are surrounded by people singing songs, by people smiling and laughing, and yet you can still feel as if no one sees you or even notices you or knows your struggles.

You can be lonely at work. You're just not connected, nor engaged in what's going on in your office. Coworkers seem to form friendships, going to lunch, and planning after-work gatherings, but you don't seem to be a part of the group. You feel as though everyone is succeeding while you are left in the dust, alone.

And you can certainly be lonely in your own home. This world is fully of lonely marriages, where you may be part of a couple, but you are more like roommates than soul mates. You don't really share life and love together anymore. Tragically, homes today are often the place where loneliness is experienced the most. Kids are lonely, spending the majority of their day engaged more with the screens on their devices than their family members. Parents and even grandparents can be extremely lonely.

Unfortunately, loneliness can come upon us at any time. Birthdays, anniversaries, and holidays are often the most joyous time of the year. However, they can also be just as easily the most difficult days of life.

It is easy during these special days to dwell on all that has been lost. We can feel as if we have no one or nothing left. Nearly every study tells us that the time between Thanksgiving and January 1 is generally the peak season of loneliness, resulting in depression, divorce, and even suicide. Loneliness is all around us, always.

And, loneliness is not a new problem; it a universal problem that has been present throughout the ages. Don't believe me? Look with me at some of the most famous songs from the past 60 years.

First, I want to take you back to the great generation of the 1940s—what was Hank Williams singing about? Williams sang, *"I'm so lonesome I could cry."*

And then let's roll and rock on to the 1950s, where we meet the one and only, Elvis Presley. Even Elvis sang about the problem of loneliness, *"Are you lonesome tonight? Do you miss me tonight? Are you sorry we drifted apart?"* Elvis knew that we all have those days and evenings of loneliness.

Recall the melancholy of the Beatles in the 1960s, singing *"All the lonely people, where do they all come from? All the lonely people, where do they all belong?"*

Fast forward to the 70s and recall Eric Carmen plaintively crooning, *"All by myself, don't want to be, all by myself."* I have a feeling that song will be stuck in your head for the rest of the day.

Well, now I really don't want to take you into the 1980s because the 80s is the worst decade of music in history. Let's be honest; music in the 80s was so bad that they had to invent MTV because the music could not stand on its own. For those of you who love the 80s, I rest my case with a lonely song from this decade. *"Here I go again on my own. Going down the only road I've ever known."* Really? Whitesnake? But I digress, and acknowledge my

Generation X son's vehement disagreement with this point.

And then dare I go to the 1990s? *"Show me the meaning of feeling lonely. Is this the feeling I need to walk with?"* You see, even the wildly popular boy band The Backstreet Boys felt loneliness.

Songs can be the soundtracks of our very lives. We love these songs about loneliness because the words resonate with us. We also love these songs because they show us that even celebrities and some heroes battle with the same feelings that we do. Anyone can experience loneliness—no one is immune.

Loneliness has been around a long time, in fact, much longer than even Hank Williams and the 1940s. I want to share with you another song about loneliness. But this song was written and sung thousands of years ago. It was penned by King David, the king over all of Israel.

David's song of loneliness can be found in Psalm 102. David begins right away with the agony of loneliness. Listen to his words in verses 1 and 2: *"Hear my prayer, O Lord; let my cry come to you! Do not hide your face from me in the day of my distress! Incline your ear to me; answer me speedily in the day when I call!"*

You can almost feel the pain jump off of the page. This psalm is real, and it is raw. David continues on in the next several verses to express to his God what he is feeling and experiencing. In this psalm, David teaches us that we must bring our true feelings to God. In fact, the subtitle of this psalm is *"A Prayer of one afflicted, when he is faint and pours out his complaint before the Lord."*

THE REALITY OF LONELINESS

If we are to find the answer to loneliness, we must first start with the reality of loneliness. And what is the reality of loneliness?

Well, loneliness has many expressions. Loneliness is being 6 years old, your first day in school and not knowing the name of a single other student in the classroom.

Loneliness is learning that your parents are getting a divorce, and you don't know which parent you will be living with in the coming days.

Loneliness is experiencing an empty nest, watching a child leave home for the last time.

Loneliness is waiting in a sterile ICU waiting room while the dearest and best, the one you love the most is fighting for life.

Loneliness is being at the top, where the buck stops, when difficult decisions must be made.

Loneliness is, at times, being single and wondering if anybody cares.

Loneliness is, at times, being married and wondering if anybody cares.

Loneliness is saying no when all the other young men and women seem to be saying yes.

Loneliness is your daughter's wedding or your spouse's funeral.

Loneliness is an empty place at the table, an empty space in the bed, and an empty place in the heart.

These are just a few of the pictures of the reality of loneliness. You can probably identify with a few of these, and your mind is undoubtedly drifting to memories of your own loneliness.

David continues in Psalm 102, by describing his loneliness in this way, *"I am like a desert owl of the wilderness, like an owl of the waste places; I lie awake; I am like a lonely sparrow on the housetop"* (Psalm 102:6–7).

Here, David gives two powerful similes to show how he feels. He compares himself to an owl alone in the wilderness and to a little sparrow alone on the roof. Sometimes, it can seem majestic to be a bird high above the earth. But here, to David, it seems they are far removed from everything. That is how he feels in this moment. It is a sad and lonely picture.

You might be able to empathize with David. You may feel like that sparrow, that little bird on the rooftop. Well, if that's you, then I have some really good news for you because Jesus said God knows every sparrow by name. And when a sparrow falls, God knows and God cares. So, if you are a lonely sparrow on the roof, then know that Jesus sees you and cares for you. In fact, Jesus goes on to say that you have so much more value than that sparrow (Matthew 6:25–34).

Never forget the love of Jesus. For loneliness is often a lack of love, which is why we all must know and experience Jesus' great love for us. He loves you. Hold on to that truth today.

But it starts by being honest with God and ourselves. Some of us need to simply admit that loneliness is real, and that there is no shame in it because we all struggle with it.

THE REASON FOR LONELINESS

Loneliness is real; but let us not stop there. Let us explore the reason for loneliness. Let us look at why we all experience loneliness at some level.

There are three basic needs in your life and in my life. One is to love and to be loved. God created us in His image, and we are designed to share intimacy, friendships, and relationships. Before the Fall and sin entered the world, Adam "walked with God" and he knew Eve intimately and completely without shame (Genesis 3:8, 2:25). Sin changed all of this, but more on that in a minute.

The second need that we all have is the need to be known. We need to know that someone loves, knows, and accepts us. We crave the need to know that people understand who we are and why we feel the way that we feel.

Lastly, there is the need to be needed. And that is significance. We want to know that we are making an impact in the world and that we are making a difference. We want to leave a legacy.

So, we all have a need to be loved, to be known, and to be needed. As we reflect on this, it seems as if everything in our world works against these three needs.

With the universal dependence on smartphones and other devices, along with the increased reliance on social media for communicating, we have quickly become the most connected generation in all of human history. But we are also the loneliest generation in all of history. We are connected, but we are also disconnected in so many different ways.

However, the reason for loneliness goes far beyond a

dependence on technology. It is not a technological problem, rather it is a theological one. At its core, loneliness comes from sin. Now, it is critical that we understand that loneliness is *not* a sin. No, loneliness is a result of sin, for sin separates us from God. Isaiah writes in Isaiah 59:2, *"But your iniquities have made a separation between you and your God, and your sins have hidden his face from you so that he does not hear."*

Sin also affects our relationships with others. Go back to the beginning with Adam and Eve. In Genesis 3, when sin entered the world, shame entered the world. Adam and Eve hid from God. Their relationship with God was forever changed. But sin did not stop there.

Sin caused separation between Adam and Eve, too. For in God's confrontation with Adam, Adam blamed Eve for his sin. Can you imagine the loneliness Eve must have felt in this moment? When sin entered the world, loneliness came with it.

Sin causes loneliness in all of us, for loneliness exposes that we all have a hole in our heart. And loneliness causes us to ask others and ourselves: How do we fill that hole?

THE RESULT OF LONELINESS

Loneliness is real. It affects all of us. Loneliness also has a reason behind it. Lastly, loneliness has a result.

That result is that loneliness leaves a giant hole in our heart. And we look for all sorts of ways to fill that hole.

Many turn to alcohol and drugs to fill the hole or perhaps to forget that it exists. In fact, one of the principal causes of alcoholism and addictions of all kinds is loneliness. Yet, all of this just leads to more emptiness. As King Solomon declared in Ecclesiastes 1:2, *"Vanity of vanities! All is vanity."* These are the words of a man who had everything, and yet realized that he truly had nothing.

Sin will often please for a season, but it always leads to destruction and despair and eventually death. It has been often said that "sin will take you farther than you want to go; it will keep you longer than you want to stay; and it will cost you far more than you want to pay."

Sin will never fill this hole in your soul. Relationships will not fill it. Money will not fill it. Power, prestige, and popularity will not help. So how does one fill this hole?

Well, this is actually the wrong question. The real and right question is, *Who will fill that hole?*

This is the very question that David wrestled with back in Psalm 102 when he cried out to God. In verse 12, the psalm takes a drastic shift. David transitions from lament to praise, for he declares, *"But you, O Lord, are enthroned forever;*

you are remembered throughout all generations. You will arise and have pity on Zion; it is the time to favor her; the appointed time has come" (Psalm 102:12–13).

David realized that God was vastly bigger than his problem. David acknowledged and praised God who is on His throne forever. But David also knew that God is not only transcendent, but He is also deeply personal. David trusted God to have pity and show favor on Zion in His perfect timing.

David knew the personal nature of His God, for as a young shepherd, he wrote the beautiful words of Psalm 23:1, *"The LORD is my shepherd; I shall not want."*

Loneliness has exposed the hole in our hearts. With whom are you filling that hole? God alone is the only One who will satisfy you.

THE SOLUTION TO LONELINESS

And loneliness affects all of us. Even Jesus experienced loneliness. Before His public ministry, Jesus spent 40 days and nights alone in the wilderness. His only company was when He went head to head with the devil (Matthew 4:1–11, Luke 4:1–13).

Jesus knew the experience of an earthly father's death. Jesus knew the experience of not having a home. In Matthew 8:20,

Jesus exclaimed, *"Foxes have holes, and birds of the air have nests, but the Son of Man has nowhere to lay his head"* (see also Luke 9:58). Jesus was betrayed by one of the 12 disciples, and Jesus was publicly denied by another one. Just before He went to the Cross, Jesus was left alone in the Garden of Gethsemane, for His disciples could not stay awake to pray for Him in His time of need (Matthew 26:36–46).

And then, Jesus suffered the most excruciating loneliness on the Cross. For the first time in all of history, He was separated from His heavenly Father. On the Cross, *"Jesus cried out with a loud voice, saying, "Eli, Eli, lema sabachthani?" that is, "My God, my God, why have you forsaken me?"* (Matthew 27:46).

And in that eternal moment, God Himself was forsaken of God. Who can fathom that? That God Himself in Christ was forsaken and alone on the Cross!

As He took on the sins of the world, Jesus took on all of the consequences of our sin, which included loneliness. Jesus faced loneliness head-on at the Cross, so that you and I never have to be alone.

For on the Cross and through the Resurrection, Jesus defeated sin, death, and loneliness forever. The veil of the temple was torn top to bottom, which symbolized that there was no longer separation between man and God. Paul writes in Colossians 1:20, *"And through him (Jesus) to reconcile to himself all things, whether on earth or in heaven, making peace by the blood of his cross."*

Through faith in Jesus, we have been reconciled or restored to right relationship with God. We are never alone again, for Jesus is with us and He has given us the promise and presence of the Holy Spirit who lives in us (1 Corinthians 3:16).

While we still struggle with loneliness, Jesus will help us. As it declares in Hebrews:

> *Since then we have a great high priest who has passed through the heavens, Jesus, the Son of God, let us hold fast our confession. For we do not have a high priest who is unable to sympathize with our weaknesses, but one who in every respect has been tempted as we are, yet without sin. Let us then with confidence draw near to the throne of grace, that we may receive mercy and find grace to help in time of need.*

Jesus walks with you, and you can draw near to Him for help in your time of need. *"Draw near to God, and he will draw near to you"* (James 4:8).

How do I remedy loneliness?

We have acknowledged that loneliness is a universal problem, and it can attack all of us in any situation. However, Jesus has provided the victory over loneliness. I want to share with you three steps to conquering loneliness—communing with God, connecting with a church, and caring for others.

COMMUNE WITH GOD

The first step to conquering loneliness is to commune with God. This is a key that we all must understand; there's a difference between loneliness and solitude. Loneliness will hurt your soul, while solitude will help your soul. Loneliness drains you, while solitude nourishes you.

During His ministry on earth, Jesus practiced solitude often, as He would separate Himself from people and go to a secluded place to pray. This place could be a mountain, a valley, or a desert. The *where* was not the critical component of this time. The *who* was all that mattered; Jesus needed to spend time alone with His Father.

Spending time alone with God in prayer and His Word was an essential discipline for Jesus. It must be the same for us. We need daily solitude with our heavenly Father. Many people are alone in life because they are not spending time alone with God.

JACK GRAHAM

In Ephesians 3:17 (NLT), Paul encourages believers, *"Then Christ will make his home in your hearts as you trust in him."* Is Christ at home in your heart? Are you at home with God?

You may want to do as my friend Bob Beaudine challenges us to do in the book, *2 Chairs*. Put an empty chair across from you and let that be for the presence of Christ. Invite Jesus into your home and meet with Him every day by reading your Bible and spending intentional time with Him. I've been seriously meeting with God for decades now, every day of my life, and it is His presence that fills my life with meaning and purpose every single day.

So, commune with God. It is never too late to invest in this eternal relationship. Spend quality time with God today. Better yet, do it right now.

If you are struggling with loneliness today, spend time with the God who knows you, loves you, and accepts you in Christ. Experience His presence today and every day. The psalmist writes, *"Delight yourself in the Lord, and he will give you the desires of your heart"* (Psalm 37:4).

Do you have a relationship with Jesus? Jesus is not someone I just talk about; He's not just someone I think about; He's someone I know! I was captivated as a teenager with the words of Jesus in John 15:15. Jesus says, *"I call you my friend."*

What a friend we have in Jesus!

CONNECT WITH A CHURCH

The second step to conquering loneliness is to connect with a local church. Jesus built the Church and He died for the Church. He established His Church to be a family of friends. As believers, we are brothers and sisters in Christ.

I encourage all Christians to have an earthly home, a church home, and a heavenly home. Do you have a church home? We tell all of our new members at Prestonwood that we are *a church to call home.* Churches are to be the most welcoming place in the entire world because Jesus is a *"friend of sinners"* (Matthew 9:11). And we are all sinners.

This also means that no church is perfect. Our earthly home and our church home will always be far from perfect. Only our heavenly home is perfect. However, we do not abandon our earthly home or our church home because of their lack of perfection. In fact, because of sin, we must rely even more on our community of brothers and sisters in Christ.

Listen to Hebrews 10:24 and 25. The Scripture says: *"And let us consider how to stir up one another to love and good works, not neglecting to meet together, as is the habit of some, but encouraging one another, and all the more as you see the Day drawing near."* The closer we get to the return of Christ, the more we're going to need each other. It's getting tougher and tougher and tougher in our time, which means we need one another even more.

CARE FOR OTHERS

The third step to conquering loneliness is to care for hurting people. The reality we all must face is that we are often lonely because we are focusing only on ourselves. When we become completely internal, we also become lonely.

I often share with those who are struggling, if you need help, then help somebody else. All around us are lonely people who need your love, who need your help. So get involved in ministries at your church and in your community where you can serve others. Take time to visit the sick. Feed the hungry. Pray for the hurting. Share God's love with children. This is what Jesus did and this is what He commands us to do.

Try giving yourself away. Jesus said in Matthew 20:28, *"The Son of Man came not to be served but to serve, and to give his life as a ransom for many."* Jesus served others and gave Himself away. Are you following in Jesus' footsteps? In your time alone with Jesus, ask Him how you can give yourself away. Surrender to Him and to His will.

Let us give ourselves away by being generous with our time, by being generous with our labor, and by being generous with our money and resources.

Proverbs 18:24 (NKJV) states, *"A man who has friends must himself be friendly, But there is a friend who sticks closer than a brother."* Many people are lonely because they build walls, rather than building bridges into people's lives. Let us build bridges to serve others and to share the Good News of Jesus with them. Let us be the friend who sticks closer than a brother.

JESUS IS THE ANSWER

The world is filled with lonely people! Remember the words of the Beatles, *"Ah, look at all the lonely people. Where do they all come from?"* Later in the song, they sing, *"Eleanor Rigby died and was buried along with her name; nobody came."* That doesn't have to be the end of your story. You can know God. You can experience the presence of Jesus in your life. And even when it comes time to die, you will not die alone because God is with you and He will come for you and take you into His presence. He will carry you to His heavenly home, your eternal home.

Jesus promised in John 14:1–3,

"Let not your hearts be troubled. Believe in God; believe also in me. In my Father's house are many rooms. If it were not so, would I have told you that I go to prepare a place for you? And if I go and prepare a place for you, I will come again and will take you to myself, that where I am you may be also."

Trust in Jesus. He conquered loneliness for you and me on the Cross. He has prepared a perfect heavenly home for all who believe by faith in Him. As Christians, we never have to be alone, for He is our Immanuel, "God with us."

chapter five

HELP! I'M GRIEVING

We have all experienced grief—seasons of incredibly intense sorrow that shake us to the core. By definition, grief means a deep and profound sadness, usually in connection with the death of a loved one; but we all know that grief can engulf us for so many reasons, so many different losses. And this deep, emotional and mental suffering is often endured alone.

You could be grieving for a child who has turned his back on God, abandoned his family, and gone his own way. You might be fighting a debilitating illness with pain that reaches into every part of your body, and you grieve. You might be grieving the loss of financial stability, the loss of a marriage or relationship, or the loss of valuable time spent in addiction or bondage.

I'm certain that everyone reading this chapter understands that our lives on earth have a beginning, and someday, an end, when we trade our mortal bodies for something much, much greater. As believers in Christ, we know without a doubt that this life on earth is temporary, our forever home with God awaits, and our deceased loved ones who knew Jesus as Lord and Savior will be there to greet us.

But here and now, in our mortal bodies, we are all too aware of the seasons of life and how quickly they fly by. Our grandparents pass away, and our parents and siblings and friends, and sometimes we must face the most unnatural loss of all, our children. As believers, we also know of the ebb and flow of life, the highs and lows—and that this is a part of grander plan that we cannot see right now.

In this life, we form bonds that are so strong we can't imagine life without the people we hold close, the marriage we worked so hard on for years and years, or the job we work so hard at every day.

And when they're gone, the pain of loss can be so overwhelming that we can't help but cry out to God—even if we know without a doubt that our loved one is with the Lord or that in the bigger picture of life, our job is just a job, not our identity.

Sadness is a normal response to loss. Persons we loved are gone. We'll never hear their voice again, their laugh, their whispers of love on this side of eternity. The financial stability we worked so hard for is shaken by the loss of a job or the downturn in a market over which we have little control. The child we trained up to love the Lord and His people has gone astray. But eternity awaits, an eternity with God, and He will dry our tears.

In Jesus' Sermon on the Mount found in Matthew 5, He gives us the Beatitudes, His promises to His followers—the meek, the pure in heart, the righteous, the persecuted, the peacemakers, the merciful. In verse 4, Jesus provides those who grieve with a special blessing: *"Blessed are those who mourn, for they shall be comforted."*

Of course, people deal with grief and recovery in their own particular time, in their own particular way. For some, though, the pain of loss becomes something much more serious. Some who have suffered a loss grieve until it is paralyzing. So it's crucial in those circumstances to remain close to the bereaved, to watch for signs that deep mourning has become a major depressive disorder.

Some psychologists talk about the stages of grief that ultimately lead to recovery for the surviving spouse, or children of a departed parent. One line of thought breaks the process down to *numbness*, which can last a few hours to a few days; *depression*, which can linger for a week to a year;

and finally, *recovery*, which often begins several months after the loved one's death.

But how do you know when intense sadness is really something much worse?

Doctors say there are warning signs.

For most people recovering from a profound loss, levels of sadness fluctuate. People with depression feel deeply, intensely sad almost all of the time.

In the depths of grief over the death of his wife, the great British writer and Christian apologist C.S. Lewis searched for words to describe his overwhelming sense of loss.

"Her absence is like the sky," Lewis finally wrote, "spread over everything."

Lewis describes the "mad midnight moments" of mourning his wife, when he questioned everything—life and death and even God. He likened the pain of losing her to an amputation.

For a surviving spouse, parent, or child, grief can feel that way—beyond measure, with no clear beginning and no end in sight. It blankets every part of the survivor's life.

Dealing with depression caused by grief often brings a lack of self-esteem or a self-loathing. A person suffering from depression might have hallucinations, or hear voices, or see things that aren't there.

Most people grieving a loss don't feel that way. And though people who are mourning might avoid social settings, they typically accept the support of loved ones. People with depression often isolate themselves from others, even relatives and close friends.

Some doctors say there is a third category—between grieving and depression—that they describe as "complicated grief."

People dealing with complicated grief have difficulty thinking about anything but their loved one's death. Often, they can't accept that the person has died, or they become increasingly bitter over their loss. Some have difficulty remembering good times and special occasions they enjoyed with their loved one, and their grieving gets worse rather than better.

Grieving the loss of someone or something of value is normal and natural. And usually we learn to live with the ache as the days, weeks and months pass. Things can trigger a relapse—an old photo, a favorite song, a place that reminds you of the loved one you've lost.

For most, healing comes eventually even if the memory of loss never goes away. But sometimes, the grief continues for weeks, months, years. It becomes a part of us. At that point, grief is moving from an emotional reaction to an addiction. That might seem harsh—most people consider an addict one of those pitiable people panhandling on big-city streets or ducking into an alley to use whatever it is that holds them captive. But addiction includes things far beyond drugs or alcohol. Simply put, we are addicted when we are controlled or consumed by a substance, thought process, activity, or emotion to an unhealthy degree.

Second Peter 2:19 tells us, "... *For whatever overcomes a person, to that he is enslaved."*

We usually don't think of grief that way, as an addiction, but without allowing yourself to heal, by hanging on to that loss, you damage your own life and the lives of those around you.

Addictions keep us from becoming the person God wants us to be. And grief can easily take over our lives.

After the death of her beloved Prince Albert, Queen Victoria famously wore black for the remaining 41 years of her life. She might have smiled at memories of their time together, laughed with her children and grandchildren, and found joy in her life. But it appears, she was forever a lonely widow, always dressed in funeral garb, a sad figure constantly reminded of the loss she suffered.

Family and friends must be alert for signs of depression or

extreme grief—lack of appetite, trouble sleeping, even talk of suicide—and seek medical help for their loved one so that he or she can be aided in overcoming loss.

The truth is, the only way to overcome paralyzing grief requires one very difficult step: We must turn our loved one or whatever loss we are grieving loose and embrace the opportunities and ministry God has set before us.

God will provide comfort to the hurting. He will wrap you up in His love, and His love will overcome the grief of this world.

WHAT DOES THE BIBLE SAY ABOUT GRIEF?

In John 11, we find Jesus grieving for the pain of loss afflicting Martha and Mary following the death of their brother, Lazarus. Jesus shared that same ache as He grieved for His friend.

Remember that while Jesus was wholly divine, He was also wholly human. And this was a family Jesus knew well. He visited them often. They were intimate friends. The Bible tells us that Jesus loved Lazarus, not just as a brother—*philo* or brotherly love—but with *agape* love, the steadfast, sacrificial love of God.

I'm sure you remember the story—how Mary and Martha sent word to Jesus that Lazarus was extremely ill, how they watched for His coming, and how Jesus purposely delayed His arrival.

But Jesus had the best of reasons for delaying. He wasn't surprised about Lazarus's illness. In John 11:4, He said, *"This illness does not lead to death."*

Instead, it provided an incredible example of God's love for His children and a powerful testimony that Jesus truly is the Son of God! He brings life!

By the time Jesus approached their family home, Lazarus had been dead for four days, and Mary and Martha were deep in mourning.

Have you ever noticed that when people mourn a serious and significant loss, their overwhelming sadness can come wrapped in anger?

Martha, never shy about speaking her mind, greeted Jesus with an accusation: *"Lord, if you had been here, my brother would not have died."*

Here's the subtext: We thought You loved us, Jesus. Why didn't You do something? Why did You ignore our pleas? Why didn't You come when we called? Was saving Lazarus just too hard for You?

Have you ever thought something like that when times were

tough, when illness came, when circumstances were so severe that you had to cry out in desperation?

"Lord, why didn't You help me when I was diagnosed with that terrible disease?" "God, why didn't You keep my parents from divorcing?" "Where were You, Lord, when I lost my job and my savings and my future?" "Father, why didn't You step in when our child rebelled against us and You and walked away from our family?"

Of course you have. And despite what you felt, God *was* with you! But sometimes, in our lowest moments, we are so focused on what we're feeling that we don't look up to see the unmistakable presence of God in our life.

Only our Lord and Savior understands absolute abandonment. As He was dying on the cross in agony and pain, He cried out to His Father, *"My God, my God, why have you forsaken me?"*

In that moment of spiritual death, when Jesus took on all of our sins, the Father turned His back on His beloved Son. But because of that incredible sacrifice for us, Jesus assures us that we will never be forsaken if we follow Him.

On this particular day, when Jesus ordered the stone removed from the front of Lazarus's grave and Martha fretted about the smell of death, He turned to her with a gentle rebuke.

"Did I not tell you that if you believed you would see the glory of God?" Jesus said.

How many of us, when things appear to be at their worst, forget about God and His promises and try to fix things ourselves? Instead, we must trust in God and give Him the glory!

And as every Christian knows, Jesus raised Lazarus from the dead, calling in a loud voice, *"Lazarus, come out."* And the dead man walked from the tomb, wrapped in his burial linen.

The plain truth is Jesus could have healed and restored Lazarus at any moment He chose. But He used this moment, surrounded by a large crowd, to show God's love for us and His awesome power. And in the moments before transforming death to life, Jesus also gave us one of the great promises in Scripture.

"I am the resurrection and the life," He tells Martha in verses John 11:25–26. *"Whoever believes in me, though he die, yet shall he live, and everyone who lives and believes in me shall never die...."*

We never discount the pain of anyone grieving a terrible loss. But we know, without a doubt, that we will be with the loved ones we've lost, soon and forever.

Psalm 46:1 says *"God is our refuge and strength, a very present help in trouble.*" As a loving father, He wants to give you comfort, peace, love, and wisdom. Healing in the midst of such pain and loss may seem impossible, but as believers, we know nothing is impossible for God.

That is God's promise to His children, a promise repeated over and over in the Bible.

In Matthew 19:26, Jesus offers this assurance that nothing —not pain, nor grief—is insurmountable for God: *"With man this is impossible, but with God all things are possible."*

HOW DO WE DEAL WITH OUR GRIEF?

Even though we know God can and will do something to lift us from the prison of pain, it doesn't mean the next day or week will be easy. The ache of loss is fresh and deep. Peter, who knew difficulty and pain in his lifetime, tells believers in 1 Peter 5:7 to *"[cast] all your anxieties on him, because he cares for you."*

But how can the God of the universe understand my loss, the darkness that never leaves me, the aching emptiness that pierces like a knife? He can, because He knows your pain firsthand.

"He was despised and rejected by men, a man of sorrows and acquainted with grief,..." Isaiah 53:3 tells us. Jesus, who knows and loves us, who empathizes with our loss and understands all we're going through, is with you every step of the way.

The point is, it's never wrong to tell God how much you hurt, how you feel, how you don't understand the pain and loss that overwhelms you. Some of the greatest prayers in the Bible come from what must be the worst moments in someone's life.

Just think about these heart-breaking words in Psalm 42:9–11:

> *I say to God, my rock: "Why have you forgotten me? Why do I go mourning because of the oppression of the enemy?" As with a deadly wound in my bones, my adversaries taunt me, while they say to me all the day long, "Where is your God?"*

But in the next verse, the writer finds strength and hope that can only come from God.

> *Why are you cast down, O my soul, and why are you in turmoil within me? Hope in God, for I shall again praise him, my salvation and my God.*

You can be honest with God about your pain, your struggles, and your suffering. We all face things in life that we can't understand. We must turn to God. He's big enough to handle any question we can ask. And He welcomes us into His presence.

For believers, losing a loved one who had a relationship with Christ will bring overwhelming sadness, but it will also bring praise and celebration. They are face to face with God!

A funeral or a cathartic "saying goodbye" gesture can provide an opportunity for comfort. It's an opportunity to grieve, and good grief is helpful for healing the emotions and moving beyond tragedy and experiencing spiritual victory.

Many Christians know the story of Charles Spurgeon, the great 19th-century English preacher. From an early age, Spurgeon attracted such huge crowds that he occasionally would ask his congregation to stay home on a Sunday morning so more visitors could hear the promises in God's Word.

With his booming voice—he once addressed a crowd of 23,000 on sheer lung power—hearty laugh and keen sense of humor, Spurgeon appeared to be at the peak of health, a man joyful and content. Instead, he suffered spiritually, emotionally, and physically for much of his life.

His spiritual suffering began roughly five years before his conversion. The son and grandson of preachers, the young Spurgeon knew of the Gospel, the Good News, but not about the personal relationship a Christian has with our Lord.

JACK GRAHAM

"The justice of God, like a ploughshare, tore my spirit," he said. "I was condemned, undone, destroyed—lost, helpless, hopeless—I thought hell was before me."

That spiritual suffering led him to reject sin and seek only the Word of God and the joy of salvation.

Soon, Spurgeon was drawing thousands of people eager to hear his message of hope. He was a mesmerizing figure as he paced across the stage, acting out Bible verses, describing the wonders of salvation and the horrific eternity awaiting those who refused to put their faith in God.

But his ministry attracted attacks and persecution, too. He had received only a modest education—there was nothing of the "proper vicar" in him—and his critics called him a demagogue, "the pulpit buffoon."

"I am perhaps vulgar, but it is not intentional, save that I must and will make people listen," Spurgeon said. "My firm conviction is that we have had enough polite preachers."

And so he soldiered on, sometimes reveling in the abuse for the sake of his Savior, but often struggling, on his knees, "with the hot sweat rising from my brow under some fresh slander poured upon me."

Outwardly, Spurgeon seemed self-assured, a preacher at

home before the largest of crowds. But inside, fear gripped him, fear that he would fail to properly bring God's Word to a world that desperately needed to hear it.

If his deacons left him even for a few minutes before a service, "they would find me in a most fearful state of sickness, produced by that tremendous thought of my solemn responsibility," Spurgeon wrote.

In October 1856, Spurgeon addressed a packed crowd of 12,000 at the Royal Surrey Gardens Music Hall, with 10,000 more filling the gardens. Suddenly, someone shouted "Fire!" and in the panic that followed, seven people died and 21 suffered serious injuries.

Spurgeon was so distraught with grief that he had to be carried from the pulpit. He was taken to a friend's home where he remained for several days, in deep depression.

"Perhaps never soul went so near the burning furnace of insanity, and yet came away unharmed," he said later of that terrible event.

But his grief-fueled depression remained, and Spurgeon would struggle with it for the rest of his life. He was also beset with a number of serious illnesses, including gout so painful "that I could no longer bear it without crying out," he wrote.

Spurgeon's physical and emotional suffering lasted to his final hour, but he never wavered in his faith. In what would be his final sermon in 1891, Spurgeon ended as he always did—by praising his Savior.

"These 40 years and more I served Him, blessed be His name, and I have had nothing but love from Him. I would be glad to continue yet another 40 years in the same dear service here below if so it pleased Him.

"His service is life, peace, joy. Oh, that you would enter on it at once! God help you to enlist under the banner of Jesus even this day! Amen."

Life brings grief and pain and suffering. But God provides the strength to endure it and thrive. Once he placed his faith in Jesus, Charles Spurgeon never wavered, no matter how pressing the pain or grief, no matter how deeply he descended into endless depression. His God was always with him.

Many believe the book of Job is the oldest book in the Bible, written perhaps seven centuries before the birth of Jesus. But even then, before God handed down the Law to Moses, before the prophets, Job had already asked *the big question*.

"*If a man dies, shall he live again?*" Job wonders in verse 14:14.

It's the question people have asked over the millennia.

Instinctively, we know there must be more than the life we've living now. People from almost every tribe and civilization believe that the death of our bodies isn't the end, but a point of transition.

For the Christian, it is a certainty. Christ is alive, and therefore we live! It's His Resurrection that is the promise of an eternity spent with God.

King David, flawed as all of us are and grieving his loss in life, was still a man after God's own heart. His failures were spectacular, but so was his faith.

In the beautiful 23rd Psalm, David's praise is as lovely as anything in literature:

> *The Lord is my shepherd; I shall not want.*
> *He makes me lie down in green pastures.*
> *He leads me beside still waters.*
> *He restores my soul.*
> *He leads me in paths of righteousness*
> *for his name's sake.*

But then, there's a change.

> *Even though I walk through the valley of the shadow*
> *of death, I will fear no evil, for you are with me;*
> *your rod and your staff, they comfort me.*

> *You prepare a table before me*
> *in the presence of my enemies;*
> *you anoint my head with oil;*
> *my cup overflows.*
> *Surely goodness and mercy shall follow me*
> *all the days of my life,*
> *and I shall dwell in the house of the* Lord *forever.*

Did you notice that? In the first verse, David speaks of God in the third person: He makes; He leads; He restores.

But when David goes through the *"valley of the shadow of death,"* he's no longer speaking of God in the third person. He is speaking directly to Him.

I always point out to people that when we walk through life's valleys and shadows, we're closer to the Lord than at any other time. We experience His presence in a totally different way.

We're no longer talking about Him; we're talking to Him.

God loves each of us intimately. He is our heavenly Father, and He promises to dry every tear. When we grieve for a loved one, God holds us close and brings peace beyond our understanding.

In the darkest moments of life, He fills our lives with hope.

For the believer, death and the toils and troubles of this life can bring us or should remind us of the incredible peace and joy of eternity!

Christ is alive, and through Him, those we have lost live, and what we lost will be restored to us!

chapter six

HELP! I'M ANGRY

We live in an angry society. Expressions of unhealthy anger are everywhere. You just need to check out the news, the Internet, or any social media platform to see the rage and fury in the world.

Anger can originate from many sources, from simple learned behavior all the way to childhood abuse. Breaking free from debilitating anger can feel like facing an unconquerable mountain. Whether anger is obvious and outward, or quiet and internal, it can become a controlling, devastating stranglehold not only of individuals, but of whole families, and even communities.

Anger is one of the basic human emotions that are part of our survival mechanism. It is a morally neutral feeling and is part of the fight-or-flight response of our nervous system. Anger triggers the release of stress hormones and prepares us to fight, but that doesn't always mean physical violence.

Focused correctly, it can be just the fuel we need to combat injustice and social wrongs.

In today's society, anger in the form of physical violence is rarely appropriate, but here are a few examples: the brave passengers aboard United Flight 93 on September 11, 2001, used anger to storm the cockpit and physically overcome the hijackers whose intention was to commit terrorism against our country; military personnel are trained to focus anger to fight wars; a witness might use anger to stop an attacker from assaulting an innocent person.

Anger only becomes unhealthy when we act inappropriately on it, or it becomes frequent because of harbored resentment. Our bodies are not designed to be constantly subjected to the stress of anger.

In the Bible, there are two kinds of anger—righteous, or godly anger, and unrighteous, or ungodly anger. We will look at both in this chapter.

Anger is everywhere! There are so many angry people, and the world is a violent and dangerous place as a result.

We shouldn't be surprised because Scripture says in the last days, perilous and scary times will come (2 Timothy 3:1–9). And it's getting pretty scary, isn't it?

JACK GRAHAM

Our whole nation seems so angry and violent. People are just mad. Many are angry all the time, and either filled with an internal rage that seethes and burns or controlled by obvious and inappropriate outbursts that can be unleashed at any moment.

Several years ago, Deb and I were out for a nice breakfast on a Saturday morning. We were driving down the street and came to a stoplight where we noticed two guys getting out of their trucks, one in front of us, one behind us, and they were shouting at each other. The next thing you know, they were doubling up and squaring off, and about to fight in the middle of the intersection.

It didn't last long. One guy took the other guy down and began kicking him in the head. Then they both just jumped back in their trucks and drove off like nothing happened! Really? On a Saturday morning, two guys just duking it out in the middle of an intersection!

What about the fights breaking out—even a death—at Popeye's Fried Chicken? People were all stirred up and fighting over a fried chicken sandwich. Are you kidding me? I mean, you've heard of road rage; well that was some chicken rage!

But anger is not always so obvious as in these instances. For many, anger is something deep down inside that has changed their personalities. They have no peace, instead a constant strife and anger that boils internally.

GODLY ANGER

There is an anger that is not sinful. It is righteous anger. Ephesians 4:26 says, *"Be angry and do not sin...."* So what is righteous anger?

Psalm 7:11 tells us that God is angry with the wicked every day, and the Bible says the wrath of God, His burning anger, is executed in judgment over unbelieving and unrepentant people. Yes, God, *who is love,* will judge all sin and all sinful people who do not repent. This is why God sent His only Son, Jesus Christ, to die on the Cross for our sins, because God is not willing that any should perish, but that all should come to repentance (2 Peter 3:9). This is the good news of the Gospel.

Yes, God, with holy wrath, will judge sinful people who do not come to find forgiveness, healing and hope in Christ— that is a fact. So if God Himself is angry with sin and sinful behavior, then it's also possible for us to have godly anger toward sin and sinful behavior.

Jesus did. He demonstrated the love of God perfectly on the Cross with His very life, yet when He saw sin in the temple, the hypocrites who were merchandising the people, He took a whip to them on two occasions. This wasn't the meek and mild Jesus you see depicted in all those old paintings. This was Jesus with a whip driving the moneychangers out of the temple, angry at the abuse going on in the holy place of worship. Jesus never sinned, so this was not sinful anger but godly, righteous anger.

There are some things that ought to make us angry, things we should stand up for. Never passive, placid, or weak, we should boldly speak the truth in love.

Like the taking of the innocent lives, millions of babies aborted in the womb of their mothers—that ought to make us angry! The pornography industry and the devastating effect it has on our society—that ought to make us angry! The persecution of Christians worldwide—that should make us angry! The cruelty of human trafficking, and the injustice of racial prejudice should make us angry! All these things, and more, ought to stir righteous indignation in the soul of the believer, enough that we would take action and fight for what is right.

These are the things we should get worked up about! Romans 12:21 tells us to overcome evil with good, and that is what God has called us to do.

UNGODLY ANGER

Unresolved anger and bitterness is often seen in the hearts of unregenerate, unbelieving people, but unfortunately it's seen in the hearts and lives of believers as well. You see, the passage in Ephesians 4 was written to believers, so unrighteous anger is a problem for everyone, it seems.

One study indicates that anger shows up in the average person's life eight to 10 times a day in some form or another. So, if you say you never get angry, you need to repent of falsehood because you *do* get angry, and so do I—I admit it. And I'm not talking about righteous anger!

As a pastor, I've discovered through the years that many people live year after year with some kind of anger, resentment or bitterness in their life. Anger is not only breaking apart our marriages and families, but our church communities and workplaces as well.

You see, anger almost certainly leads to disobedience, which is a very serious matter. In fact, Moses, God's chosen leader, never saw the Promised Land because he lost his composure in anger, and as a result, didn't follow the Lord's instructions. In Numbers 20, Moses was faced, for the second time, with a whining crowd of Israelites who were thirsty. Now previously, the Lord had instructed Moses to strike a rock once, and it yielded water. But this time, He was told to speak to the rock. Moses was so angry with the grumbling mob that he struck the rock twice, forgetting his instructions. The symbolism behind this story is another subject entirely, but here we see the seriousness of Moses' anger. It caused him to miss out on entering the Promised Land!

Ungodly anger can cause us to miss out on God's best blessings, just as it did for Moses.

THE ANATOMY OF ANGER

If you're reading this chapter and you're struggling with anger, welcome to the human race! There is hope in Jesus Christ, and freedom can be yours this very day. The uncontrollable anger that so many people feel on a frequent, even constant basis, is so devastating; but God has a solution in Ephesians chapter 4. Let's take a look, verse by verse.

THE STARTING POINT OF ANGER

> *Be angry and do not sin; do not let the sun go down on your anger, ...* —Ephesians 4:26

This is where we can halt anger in its tracks before it takes a deeper root. Simply put, just don't go to bed without resolving disagreements that have led to angry feelings.

When there is an underlying issue that needs to be resolved, this may be more easily said than done. But in many situations, it may be as simple as resolving quarrels that arise straight away with humility and maturity.

We can't control how other people respond, but as much as you can admit your mistakes, apologize and move forward, the better. This always makes it easier for the other person to do the same. Maybe it doesn't resolve perfectly the way you would like, but lingering angry feelings can melt away just by focusing on Jesus, His forgiveness for all your sins, and everything He's done for you.

THE PROGRESSION OF ANGER

... and give no opportunity to the devil.
—Ephesians 4:27

If we don't deal with it straight away, unresolved anger will open the door of your heart, your life, your home, and family to the power of the Enemy and to the bondage of Satan himself. Yes, there are satanic strongholds in people's lives, and it is anger that opens the door.

If the devil literally knocked on your door, would you let him in? Would you allow him to sleep in your bed? I'm sure you would say, "Absolutely not!" But if you do let the sun go down without resolving anger and bitterness, you are essentially giving him an opportunity to invade your world, even establish a beachhead where all the artillery of hell can be unleashed against you, your family and everyone around you!

You see, hell is full of anger, gnashing of teeth, wrath and judgment; and when you give Satan a place in your life because of anger, you're inviting all hell into your house.

On the other hand, heaven is a place where we are forgiven and cleansed in Christ. When you invite Christ in to cleanse your home and cleanse the temple of your life, then all of heaven comes in.

THE CLAMOR OF ANGER

> *Let no corrupting talk come out of your mouths, but only such as is good for building up, as fits the occasion, that it may give grace to those who hear.*
> —Ephesians 4:29

Clamor means "loud speaking or noisy shouting," and is generally accompanied by profanity and cursing. Many people grow up in this kind of environment, and it is the origin of unhealthy anger habits. Children who grow up with shouting, arguing, hatefulness, and spitefulness not only learn to emulate the same behavior, but become uncontrollably bound to it.

Maybe you recognize that you grew up in that environment, and you're not in full control of your tongue. All hope is not lost! James 3:2–5 talks about this very issue.

> *For we all stumble in many ways. And if anyone does not stumble in what he says, he is a perfect man, able also to bridle his whole body. If we put bits into the mouths of horses so that they obey us, we guide their whole bodies as well. Look at the ships also: though they are so large and are driven by strong winds, they are guided by a very small rudder wherever the will of the pilot directs. So also the tongue is a small member, yet it boasts of great things.*

James goes on to talk about how the tongue is a fire, a world of unrighteousness, and how it can stain our whole body. You see, our tongue sets the course of our entire life, and if we allow it, "will be set on fire by hell."

The answer is wisdom from above. If we seek His wisdom, which is pure, peaceable, gentle, open to reason, full of mercy and good fruits, impartial and sincere, the harvest of righteousness will be ours.

So don't expose your family to filthy talk. Set up your children for emotional success, not failure. Let the Holy Spirit be the bit in your mouth and seek His wisdom to control your tongue.

THE GRIEF OF ANGER

> *And do not grieve the Holy Spirit of God, by whom you were sealed for the day of redemption.*
> —Ephesians 4:29

How do you grieve the Holy Spirit? You can only grieve a person, right? You might say, "I thought the Holy Spirit was a powerful force and an influence in our lives." Actually, the Holy Spirit is a *person*—the third person of the Trinity. God, the Father; God, the Son; and God, the Holy Spirit. He is the Comforter and the Counselor who has come, empowering us, and equipping us. But the Holy Spirit is a person, not an "it" or an "influence."

Can God, the Holy Spirit be grieved? Yes! When we let the devil in, the Holy Spirit who lives within us grieves and weeps.

The word *grieve* is a love word. You can only grieve someone who loves you. You can hurt someone's feelings, but you can't really grieve them unless love is in the equation. So, because God loves us and because of our relationship with Him in Jesus Christ, when we are angry and hostile, full of hate and bitterness, and have left the door wide open for the Enemy, it grieves the Holy Spirit deeply.

THE RAGING FIRE OF ANGER

> *Let all bitterness and wrath and anger and clamor*

> *and slander be put away from you, along with all malice.* —Ephesians 4:31

So here it all comes together—once we've let the sun go down, let the devil get a foothold, grieved the Holy Spirit, this is where we end up: Bitterness—a seething rage within.

I've known many people who are embittered about circumstances in their lives, problems they're facing, being hurt by someone. I've known people who are bitter with God, the church, or themselves. For a myriad of reasons, they're bitter people.

Bitterness is deep within—an inside job. According to Hebrews 12:15, it's described as a root. A root goes down deep, unseen. But the *fruit* of bitterness is outrageous, inappropriate behavior that is very visible in a person's life.

Then notice what happens beyond bitterness—wrath! This is the burning, the agitation and the aggravation that is constantly churning inside. And it doesn't take but a spark to get a fire going.

I have my own personal parable about this I'd like to share:

I have a fire pit, and I was trying to burn up some wood because my wood pile had become a home for rats and other varmints. Now I failed Boy Scouts, yes, actually failed.

I'm just not very good at this kind of thing. But here I was, burning up the wood and I got a really good fire going. Of course, I cheated—I used fire starters.

I decided to throw another log on, and because I just tossed it in, sparks flew everywhere. The next thing you know, my yard was on fire! Well, not the whole yard, but I got a decent grass fire going. Thankfully, there was a garden hose right next to me and I put that fire out before it did too much damage.

So this is the parable of the burning logs: A person carrying around wrath is like a person carrying a raging fire on the inside. All it takes is for somebody to carelessly throw a log on it, by doing or saying the wrong thing, and the next thing you know, sparks are flying everywhere. Now you've got a fire in the yard that could burn the house down! You've got to put that thing out.

So there's bitterness, wrath, and now real anger. It shows up on your whole countenance. There are no signs of joy, no evidence of peace, just a scowl. The fight-or-flight hormones kick in. You clench your fists; your body shakes; your face gets red; and your eyes narrow. While problems such as anxiety or depression drain you emotionally and physically, anger is the opposite, and the adrenaline kicks in. Now you're ready to fight somebody! The devil's not only in bed; he's pulling up the covers.

Next is clamor—loud speaking or shouting. Voices get raised, and profanities start flying. Do you think this grieves the Holy Spirit? Of course it does.

I'm sure any married couple knows how it can be. Deb and I have had some arguments, or at least strong discussions, that you can hear several blocks away! But there is a big difference between a disagreement and straight outrage and abusiveness. Whatever you do, don't let your kids be exposed to this.

Then it talks about slander—put it away from you! I've noticed that people who are angry all the time like to tell other people about it, and it typically comes with slander, lies and gossip. You're never more like the devil than when you're slandering people because his very name means "the accuser" or "the slanderer."

You'd think this would be enough, but the devil's not done yet.

Next is malice, which means "ill will." This is the culmination of the whole progression, and what turns people into mad men and mad women. This is when people are ready to hit somebody, or jump out of a truck and duke it out! This is where normal people become bullies with words, or even worse, actually hit their spouse or abuse a child. God help anybody who gets to this stage because now they are totally in bondage to the power of Satan.

THE BONDAGE OF ANGER

Look how far it progresses, all because anger was not dealt with back at the start. We should be dealing with anger long before it gets to this point, when the sun was coming up and going down.

Have there been too many suns going up and down since you dealt with your anger? If you don't deal with it now, it's going to progress like this, all the way to where you are in bondage to the power of the devil, and you just can't control yourself anymore.

I'm telling you, deal with it now, because you don't know what Satan can do with a lie. He can take that fire and add a tiny spark. Before you know it, everything is burning down.

Anger—it's no way to live. It can actually kill you, or worse, someone else. So I ask you: Is your anger worth dying for?

GOD'S ANSWER FOR ANGER

> *Be kind to one another, tenderhearted, forgiving one another, as God in Christ forgave you.*
> —Ephesians 4:32

How has God in Christ forgiven us? Totally and completely.

But how can I forgive?

So many people have been hurt, wronged or terribly abused. You might be saying "You just don't know what that person did to me." And I've had many people tell me that they couldn't stop thinking and obsessing over some awful thing that happened in their past, and they just couldn't forgive the offender, even when they knew that it was wrong not to.

But you know what they did to Jesus? He was completely innocent, and they stripped Him bare, mocked Him, cursed Him and spat on Him. They beat Him within an inch of His life, and they nailed Him to a cross—God's pure and perfect Lamb!

He voluntarily laid down His life and gave it into the hands of sinful men. And He did it for us—for your sins and mine.

While Jesus was on the cross, some of the first words that He said were, *"Father, forgive them for they know not what they do"* (Luke 23:34). That's forgiveness—total and complete forgiveness.

The word *forgive* actually means "to pay a debt." You see, we owed a debt we could not pay, and Jesus paid a debt He did not owe—ours.

Forgiving isn't endorsing.

Let me say this loud and clear. Forgiving someone is not saying that what they did was okay, and it is by no means endorsing the behavior or even letting them off the hook. In fact, if someone has done something to you that was a criminal offense, let the authorities handle it.

When my dad was brutally murdered in 1970, I wanted the authorities to bring the offender to justice. And I knew I had to forgive my father's murderer, or my own life would be ruined from having bitterness and anger in my heart. How could I love my wife, my family, and my church with a heart tainted with anger and unforgiveness?

The Bible says we are to let God be the judge. Let God judge that person who broke your heart! Let God judge that person who abused you! Let God be God!

Romans 12:19 says, Beloved, never avenge yourselves, but leave it to the wrath of God, for it is written, *"Vengeance is mine, I will repay, says the Lord."*

So we just have to make a decision to exercise our faith and trust that He is the best judge to bring perfect justice.

Forgiveness is about you.

Forgiveness is not about the other person anyway; it's about you. And when you forgive someone, you set the captive free, and the captive you set free is *you*!

God is saying, "I want to exchange My love, forgiveness and

kindness for your rage, bitterness, and pain." That's a great deal, because now you're no longer living in the chains of the past, the bondage of the devil is broken, and the pain of the circumstances will be able to melt away. You can live truly free when you forgive as God in Christ has forgiven you.

Repentance is the key.

You can break free of the bondage of anger. How? It starts with repentance. That means you change the way you think about the situation. You admit and own it. You can't repent for somebody else, but you can repent for yourself.

Confess it—don't nurse it, rehearse it, and don't converse it by talking about it all the time. Any moment you're focused on the hurt and the pain, that's another day that you go to bed angry. Get your eyes off the person who wronged you and get your eyes on Jesus! Obsess over Him, and the same God who has forgiven you will also free you from the stronghold of anger by the power of the Holy Spirit.

It's easy to say, "That's unnatural." Absolutely! It's the supernatural work of God in your life.

chapter seven

HELP! I'M DEPRESSED

In 2009, I was given six words that changed my life. These words were spoken by a close friend during one of the greatest trials I had ever faced. My spirit was low; my body was tired, and I was unsure of what was next. These words were "You are going to be okay."

Here is what happened. I had recently been diagnosed with prostate cancer. Before this diagnosis, I was very healthy, and I had never had a major illness in my life. Then, all of a sudden, the doctor told me that I have cancer. I was completely caught off guard, but I still felt prepared in some ways.

I actually felt strangely ready for the ensuing surgery and the follow-up. I was spiritually prepared. I was ready to go. I was ready to get this over and done. This is how I often operated; when confronted with a problem, I would power through with faith, optimism, and courage.

And so, I had the surgery to remove the cancer. I didn't tell many people; I didn't tell our church family so as not to concern them. In fact, I checked in to the hospital under a different name because I did not want anybody to know that I was even in the hospital, much less having a serious surgery.

The surgery went well, and the doctors claimed that it was very successful. I was grateful to hear the news and truly believed I was ready to get going. But suddenly, things changed drastically. Doctors questioned whether or not they had removed all the cancer, and this really rocked my world.

I realized I was now in for a bigger battle than I thought. This would not only be a physical battle, but also a spiritual and emotional battle. In the ensuing days and weeks, I was pulled into a valley of anxiety and depression. There were many sleepless nights, and my mind raced with terrible fears and worries that I'd never experienced before in my life.

My family was amazing, and my wife, Deb, stood by me and supported me the whole way. The church gave me time off to heal and recover. But even after this time off, I wasn't ready to go; something was just not right. I felt as though I would never return to normal.

I began to realize that I was dealing with something that was life-altering in many ways. During the sleepless nights, there was one question that I kept asking Deb, "Am I going to be okay?" I would then wonder to myself, "Am I going to get through this? Am I stuck like this?"

Eventually, I received much-needed help for the depression I found myself experiencing. I'll expound more about that later.

I wanted to share my story at the outset of this chapter as a reminder that we all need God's help every day. We were not meant to do life alone. We need the help of God and the help of others.

We need God's help because we live in depressing times! Just watch the news. It does not matter when you read this because let us be honest, the news is always depressing. Would you agree? When I watch the news, I am reminded of Paul's words to Timothy in 2 Timothy 3:1, when he says, *"But understand this, that in the last days there will come times of difficulty."* In the next several verses, Paul paints a bleak and nasty picture of the world during these last days.

So, in many ways, we should not be surprised at the depressing news and the depressing state of affairs that is in our world today.

But what about your own world? What are you going through right now? Perhaps, you have a child who has rebelled and run away. Perhaps, it feels as if your marriage is on the edge.

Perhaps, you have experienced the loss of a beloved spouse. Perhaps you are facing serious financial or health problems. Perhaps, like me, you have even asked yourself, "Am I going to be okay? Am I going to get through this?"

We all experience struggles. And, more and more, depression is one of the biggest struggles that many people deal with in our culture. Depression has been called the common cold of emotional illness for several reasons. But depression is not like a cold that you know will run its course and you'll feel better in a handful of days. People struggle with depression for weeks, months, years. Everyone is wired differently. Everyone's struggle is different.

One reason depression is called the common cold of emotional illness is because of the sheer numbers; it affects 20 million adults (and many more teenagers and younger) in America. Depression will break you down. It will burn you out. And it will bring struggles that you can barely describe. Secondly, no one is immune from depression. Even spiritual leaders and devout Christians struggle with it. As a matter of fact, some of the great men and women of Christian and biblical history have suffered from depression.

WHAT DOES THE BIBLE SAY ABOUT DEPRESSION?

I want to introduce you to a man that we'll meet in the

Scripture here named Elijah. He was a powerful prophet of God, one who was used by God to bring amazing and miraculous victories. Yet even this mighty prophet fell into a fit of deep depression. He would actually become so distraught that he prayed he would die. In 1 Kings 19, we read his story.

> *Ahab told Jezebel all that Elijah had done, and how he had killed all the prophets with the sword. Then Jezebel sent a messenger to Elijah, saying, "So may the gods do to me and more also, if I do not make your life as the life of one of them by this time tomorrow." Then he was afraid, and he arose and ran for his life and came to Beersheba, which belongs to Judah, and left his servant there. But he himself went a day's journey into the wilderness and came and sat down under a broom tree. And he asked that he might die, saying, "It is enough; now, O Lord, take away my life, for I am no better than my fathers."* —1 Kings 19:1–4

This is a powerful and unique story! And it is far from over. Let me first give you the background for this story from Scripture.

Just a few days before, Elijah—this great prophet of God—stood upon Mount Carmel against all of the false prophets of Baal (1 Kings 18). He was outnumbered 850 to 1. Talk about no chance.

But Elijah had God on his side. He called down fire from heaven, and the fire consumed the altar built in dedication to the one true God. Elijah destroyed and defeated these enemies of God and his people. This was a time of victory and celebration for Elijah and all of the Israelites. God singularly used this man of God, Elijah, as His instrument in a mighty and amazing way.

Well, when the cruel and wicked Queen Jezebel heard what happened on Mount Carmel, she threatened the life of this great prophet of God. Yet, this time Elijah did not stand firm in his faith. Instead of being strong and confident in his God, Elijah ran for his life. He became fearful, anxious, and afraid. Elijah fled and ran more than 30 miles into the desert, and there he prayed, *"O Lord, let me die."*

When I read this story, I am so grateful that God tells us in His Word the true and full stories of His saints. Just like you and me, Elijah (and others) who faithfully served the Lord God, faced deep spiritual and emotional problems. This reveals a great truth. You can be physically healthy and even spiritually healthy, and still be emotionally and mentally fatigued.

Let me put it another way. You can be completely healthy on the outside, and still be deeply depressed on the inside.

JACK GRAHAM

THE WHOLE STORY OF OUR HEROES IN THE FAITH

It is easy for us to put these great men and women of God on a pedestal. However, the Bible includes stories such as Elijah's to remind us that even our faith heroes have great struggles, just as you and I do.

And it was not just Elijah who struggled with depression. Moses experienced depression to the degree that he was ready to give up on life, as he was overwhelmed by leading the people of Israel. Moses prayed to God, *"I am not able to carry all this people alone; the burden is too heavy for me. If you will treat me like this, kill me at once ..."* (Numbers 11:14–15).

The same thing happened to Jonah after his experience in the great fish. He saw an amazing revival, but he actually became angry at God. He could not understand how God would show mercy on these miserable Ninevites. He was an angry, pouting prophet. As a result of his self-pity and his anger, he fell into a depression; and in Jonah 4:3, he prayed, *"O Lord, please take my life from me, for it is better for me to die than to live."*

And, of course, there is David—the man after God's own heart. He was one of the greatest men who ever lived, a king, and a mighty and powerful warrior for God. And yet, David, who gave us so many of the psalms under the inspiration of the Holy Spirit, often expressed his hurt, his pain, his depression, and his anxiety in the Scripture. That is why so many of us who have been through a time of depression run to the psalms. The psalms comfort and challenge us at the same time.

RUN TO THE PSALMS

We identify with David in the psalms because he writes as one who knows deep pain and sorrow. As you read them, you hear the heart of someone who is broken. But you also read that God is near to the brokenhearted (Psalm 34:18).

Psalm 13:1–4 a classic example of depression in the life of David. And I thank God that he preserved this psalm just for us. Read and meditate on these powerful first four verses, *"How long, O Lord? Will you forget me forever? How long will you hide your face from me? How long must I take counsel in my soul and have sorrow in my heart all the day? How long shall my enemy be exalted over me? Consider and answer me, O Lord my God; light up my eyes, lest I sleep the sleep of death, lest my enemy say, 'I have prevailed over him,' lest my foes rejoice because I am shaken."*

These verses are such a vivid picture of the pit of depression. This is what the low point looks like for David. Go back and read those verses again. David cannot get away from the question: How long will this last? Four times in just these verses, David asks God, "how long." David wants to know if he will ever be okay. He wants to know if he is going to make it through this.

But David turns the corner in verse 5. Here is how he closes this psalm, *"But I have trusted in your steadfast love; my heart shall rejoice in your salvation. I will sing to the Lord, because he has dealt bountifully with me"* (Psalm 13:5–6).

Do you want to turn the corner as David did? David was overcome and overwhelmed by this depression and this despondency in his life, and yet he learned to trust in God again. He learned to rejoice and to sing praises to his God again.

Just like David, there is hope for you and for me. Do not give up, for you can turn the corner, too. God will help you through this. He will sustain you and strengthen you. And one way that we can all experience God's daily help is to run to psalms such as Psalm 13.

HOW DOES THIS APPLY TO ME?

Depression can often make us feel defeated, as if we will never get up again. But I want you to know that there is victory in Jesus. Jesus defeated sin, death, and, yes, depression on the Cross and through the Resurrection. In fact, just before He was to be crucified, Jesus taught His disciples at the Last Supper, *"... In the world you will have tribulation. But take heart; I have overcome the world"* (John 16:33).

There is victory in Jesus, and I want to share how all of us can experience His victory over depression. It is not always easy, but I promise that Jesus will help you and walk with you every step of the way. Here are my six antidotes for depression:

1. Trust God's Promises

I wrote earlier in this book that I would share about how I got help for my depression. Well, let me take you back to the summer of 2009. I had been diagnosed with prostate cancer and was recovering from surgery. I had taken off a couple of months and I tried to return in September. But it was very clear to me that I was still not ready. In fact, for the first time in my life, I was unable to complete a sermon due to health reasons.

All I can remember is that I was just extremely tired. Always tired. I woke up tired. I walked tired. I could barely work at all. In fact, one of my biggest problems was that I struggled to read or study! That had never happened before in my life!

So how was I going to preach if I couldn't prepare? I knew that I needed the promises of God! Perhaps, more than ever before, I needed God's promises.

I delved into my sermon files, and I chose messages that I had preached in the past on God's promises. These were promises that I needed and believed that others needed as well. I decided to walk by faith and to stand on the promises of God, and to trust that He would get me through the difficult season. I was trusting God to help me turn this corner.

At the time, I was just trying to survive. I hadn't considered how the sermon series would be received. The interesting thing is that when *PowerPoint Ministries* later carried these messages on radio and television, this series on God's promises had the greatest reach and response of any sermon series that I had ever done.

And I am telling you, those were the weakest days of my life, in every way. But it became clearer and clearer that people all over the world desperately need God's promises to hold on to during the dark and difficult days of life. No wonder the Apostle Paul says in 2 Corinthians 12:10, "... *For when I am weak, then I am strong.*"

This is one of the most important truths that you can learn during your depression. It is what I call the upside-down nature of the Christian life. When you are weak, you learn to trust in God's strength. That is the complete opposite of what you would think, but it is true. You become strong—although your strength will fail, you will be living in God's strength, which will never fail.

In Psalm 119:67, the psalmist declared, "Before I was afflicted I went astray, but now I keep your word." This can happen to you. You can trust in God's Word. Scripture is full of God's promises, which will help you find strength and comfort during this time of weakness and despair.

2. Exchange the Lies for God's Truth

Always remember that depression is a lie! Peter reminds us to, *"Be sober-minded; be watchful. Your adversary the devil prowls around like a roaring lion, seeking someone to devour"* (1 Peter 5:8). Satan is always looking to attack us at our weakest point. That is what he did with Jesus in the wilderness (Matthew 4, Luke 4). And his battle plan has not changed.

During my depression, I can remember all the lies that the Enemy would whisper to me. There were so many false thoughts about my identity and my purpose. During times of depression, many people feel worthless and weak because they are listening to the lies of Satan.

Exchange the lies for the truth! That is why we must memorize God's Word. God's Word is our sword, which is the only offensive weapon we have in God's armor (Ephesians 6:17). When Jesus was attacked by Satan in the wilderness, He always responded with God's Word. Jesus had His sword ready and pointed against His Enemy. We must follow in His perfect example.

When Satan comes against you, when his lies fill your mind,

pull out your Bible and battle the lies with God's truth. Study and meditate on what God says about you in His Word! You are a child of God! You are stronger than you think! And never forget that God will fight for you.

Now, sometimes it is just a matter of putting one foot in front of the other. It is about getting up when you feel like lying down. But even this teaches us that we do not live based on our feelings. We listen to them, yes, but we do not always trust them. I often remind others and myself that we do not feel our way into acting, we act our way into feeling. And that is true faith.

3. Discover God's Mission

Do you know what many people experiencing depression need? You need a new mission in your life. Do not waste this season. There is a reason even for this dreadful season. King Solomon wrote in Ecclesiastes 3:1, *"For everything there is a season, and a time for every matter under heaven ...."* There is a reason for every season that God brings your way, even a season of depression.

You see, God is using this season of life, whatever it is, to use you and to prepare to use you in a greater way in the future. During my bout with depression, I had a close friend tell me, "Jack, I'm praying that you will learn everything you need to know from this experience." That was really good advice.

God has a mission and a plan for you. And I pray that God's promise in Jeremiah 29:11 will encourage you, as it has encouraged me time after time. God promises, *"For I know the plans I have for you, declares the Lord, plans for welfare and not for evil, to give you a future and a hope."*

God has a future and a hope for you. If you're a follower of Jesus Christ, He gives beauty for ashes. Sorrow comes for the night, but joy comes in the morning. God has a great future for you.

I know that it can be hard, but trust in God right now. And I mean truly trust Him—always. Trust Him and the promise of Romans 8:28 that *"for those who love God all things work together for good, for those who are called according to his purpose."* Trust the Good Shepherd and the promise of Psalm 23:4 that *"even though I walk through the valley of the shadow of death, I will fear no evil, for you are with me; your rod and your staff, they comfort me."*

4. Find Your Community

I cannot emphasize this enough—we need community. Reach out to your brothers and sisters in Christ. Do not fall into the trap of isolation. It feels easier to just withdraw, but in times of need, we must lean into God and lean on His family.

We all need support and encouragement, and God designed us to be in community. That is why being involved and connected to a local church is so important. If there is one place people ought to be able to come when they are hurting, it is God's Church and God's people. I know that there is no such thing as a perfect church. But God will use a broken church, just as He uses broken people.

In the past, the Church has not always been the most welcoming place for hurting people. But I truly believe that is changing in our day. I see more and more churches around the world that are ministering to the hurting. I am seeing more Christians take seriously God's command in Galatians 6:2 to *"Bear one another's burdens, and so fulfill the law of Christ."*

We were never meant to carry our burdens alone. God created the Church to be a place where we are all in this together.

5. Seek Wise Counsel

Then, there is the critical need of therapy. Yes, I mean professional therapy. I know that there has been a stigma in the Church regarding this, but I believe that as Christians, we are growing and maturing in this area. If you had a physical ailment or illness, what would you do? You would go see a doctor or specialist. Well, if you have an emotional ailment or illness, your response should be the same. You should go see a doctor, a Christian counselor, or a specialist.

Again, let me also say there is nothing wrong with medication. If you had issues with your cholesterol, I know that you would take the appropriate measure to get it fixed. Therefore, if you have emotional instability and chemical imbalances, then trust the wisdom and guidance of good professional doctors and counselors. Medication is rarely the entire part of the solution; and, as we know, it has the potential for us to overly rely upon it. However, it can often be a part of our healing. So, get the therapy you need, and that includes talk, not just medication.

Your healing should also include spiritual help from your pastor or your local church's staff. Schedule a meeting with a church leader, and share with him or her what is going on in your life. Ask that minister for wisdom, and above all, ask for prayer. As the Proverbs tell us, *"Where there is no guidance, a people falls, but in an abundance of counselors there is safety"* (Proverbs 11:14).

6. Share Your Story

As God begins to heal you, He will give you a story. He will give you a testimony. The healing will take time, and often, God will call us to share our story before His healing is complete.

Think back to Elijah. After his bout with depression in 1 Kings 19, God called Elijah to a new work and to a new calling in his life. And he got up from that desert; God used Elijah in a mighty way and in a new way. Some of you are in the midst of God's healing right now, and you need to hear that He has a new calling and a new challenge for you. God wants you to share with others what He has done in you.

In our world today, there are so many ways in which you can share your testimony. I encourage you to start at your church. Start small. Share with your small group what God has been teaching you during this season. God may grow this and give you a platform far bigger than you could imagine. My good friend and pastor Levi Lusko has said that "God wants to turn your pain into a platform, and your mess into a message."

God will heal you, and He will help you through this season. Do not give up; look for ways in which God is using this for your good and His glory. Yes, God will use even depression for good. Remember the words of Joseph in Genesis 50:20, *"As for you, you meant evil against me, but God meant it for good…."* Never forget that God will use even this for good!

A WORD OF ENCOURAGEMENT

I want to close with a final word of encouragement from the Apostle Paul. He writes in 2 Corinthians 1:3–4, *"Blessed be the God and Father of our Lord Jesus Christ, the Father of mercies and God of all comfort, who comforts us in all our affliction, so that we may be able to comfort those who are in any affliction, with the comfort with which we ourselves are comforted by God."*

God will bring you comfort and mercy in this time. And He will use you to help others. When you have been broken, you want to help other people put the pieces back together. God will give you a greater desire to pray for people, to love people, and to serve them. I tell you, I am a better Christian, a better pastor, a better counselor, a better helper, and a better person because of this experience in my life. And God will do the same in you.

chapter eight

HELP! I'M TEMPTED

Temptation is not new to mankind. Whether man or woman, young or old, having a nature that can be tempted with sin is part of the fall from grace. Temptation comes under many guises: sexual sin, shopping, food, fame, or finances to name a few. Temptation is the drive-through milkshake when we feel hungry, but know we need to lose weight. Temptation is the pop-up ad for a new pair of cool shoes when we don't feel good about our appearance, but know we have substantial credit card debt. Temptation is seeing the ethical corner we can cut to possibly get that new promotion. Temptation is being overly flattered by the flirtations of someone other than our spouse.

This is how I define temptation: It's the enticement, the solicitation, the opportunity to fulfill a natural, normal, God-given desire in a God-forbidden way.

Several years ago, Deb and I traveled to Greece and

visited the sites of ancient cities such as Ephesus, Corinth, Thessalonica, and Philippi. In the midst of our travels, we came to a spectacular place called Meteora, sheer-faced mountains topped by medieval monasteries. Perhaps you recall their isolation and majesty from the James Bond movie, *For Your Eyes Only*.

About a thousand years ago, these natural wonders of the world became a place of seclusion for monks and hermits. This group of dedicated followers of Christ were determined to get away from the world and devote their lives to prayer. They built their magnificent monasteries on the tops of these mountain peaks, as if to attempt to get as close to God and as removed from the world as possible. Yet even in their seclusion, they struggled just as we do. Depicted in paintings on the walls were expressions of suffering and pain, trials and temptations. Even those solitary monks still faced temptation.

It just goes to show that no matter where you go in life or how old or young you are, you will face temptation.

Maybe you've been walking on the mountaintops for Christ, but suddenly you're overcome with thoughts that were part of your BC years—your *before Christ* years. Now you're feeling discouraged, even defeated. You can never rest, thinking you are removed from temptation. In fact, the more determined you are to follow Christ, the more you may find yourself tempted.

If you're struggling with temptation, don't be discouraged. Every one of us is tempted throughout our lives; and being saved does not make us immune. Even the apostle Paul struggled with temptation. Romans 7:19 contains a powerful testimony on his battle with sin: *"For I do not do the good I want, but the evil I do not want is what I keep on doing."* And in Romans 7:24 he even said, *"Wretched man that I am! Who will deliver me from this body of death?"*

Sound familiar? We are all in the troughs of temptation!

The Bible says in Hebrews 4:15, even Jesus Himself *"who in every respect has been tempted as we are, yet without sin."* And that is the key; being tempted is not sin; but yielding to the temptation or dwelling upon it with our thoughts *is* sin. The first thing we need to understand is that we can't overcome our sinful nature and the power of temptation just by positive thinking and promising to do better. That's just not going to cut it. The only way to overcome temptation is through wisdom and faith.

So, as believers, why are we tempted? A. B. Simpson, a great Christian of yesteryear, said:

> Temptation exercises our faith and teaches us to pray. It is like a military drill and a taste of battle for a young soldier. It puts us under fire and compels us to exercise our weapons and prove their potency. It shows us the recourse of Christ and the preciousness of the promises of God. Every victory gives us new confidence in our victorious leader and new courage for the next onslaught of the foe.

For believers, temptation should encourage our absolute dependence upon God.

When God opens the windows of heaven to bless us, Satan often opens the windows of hell to blast us. Every spiritual commitment will be challenged in our walk with Christ, so God uses temptation for good. Martin Luther, the reformer, once said, "One Christian who has been tempted is worth a thousand who haven't."

In Matthew 4, after Jesus was baptized with the Holy Spirit, He was tested in the wilderness by Satan. It's almost a guarantee that after we have some great spiritual experience, we will find ourselves in the middle of a spiritual attack, because the devil always wants to try to steal the Word that was planted, as we see in the parable in Mark 4:14–20.

When you overcome temptation, you are fortified in your faith and strengthened in your life with Christ. Satan uses temptation to bring us down; God uses temptation to build us up. Every temptation gives us the opportunity to experience God's faithfulness and power in our lives. So, let's learn how we can use what Satan seeks to ensnare us with for the good that God intends for us.

WHAT DOES THE BIBLE SAY ABOUT TEMPTATION?

We are essentially a three-part being: body, soul, and spirit. We have physical life—that's our body, our flesh. We have soul or psychological life, which consists of our mind, will, and emotions. And if we are in Christ, we have a spiritual life.

So, the flesh connects with the world around us physically. The soul connects to the world within us through our mind, will, and emotions. The spirit relates to the invisible world above us and around us—the spiritual world.

God's purpose for us as described in 1 Thessalonians 5:23 is that we be made pure, *"your whole spirit and soul and body be kept blameless...."*

Let's take a look at Matthew 4:1–11 and revisit the temptations that were leveled at Jesus when He faced the devil in the wilderness. The three-pronged attack that came wave after wave against Christ is also used against us today. The father of lies still seeks to seduce us with the tactical assaults on our body, soul, and spirit.

> Then Jesus was led up by the Spirit into the wilderness to be tempted by the devil. And after fasting forty days and forty nights, he was hungry. And the tempter came and said to him, "If you are the Son of God, command these stones to become loaves of bread." But he answered, "It is written, 'Man shall not live by bread alone, but by every word that comes from the mouth of God.'"

> Then the devil took him to the holy city and set him on the pinnacle of the temple and said to him, "If you are the Son of God, throw yourself down, for it is written, 'He will command his angels concerning you,' and 'On their hands they will bear you up, lest you strike your foot against a stone.'"

> Jesus said to him, "Again it is written, 'You shall not put the Lord your God to the test.'" Again, the devil took him to a very high mountain and showed him all the kingdoms of the world and their glory. And he said to him, "All these I will give you, if you will fall down and worship me." Then Jesus said to him, "Be gone, Satan! For it is written, 'You shall worship the

Lord your God and him only shall you serve.'"

Then the devil left him, and behold, angels came and were ministering to him.

TEMPTATIONS OF THE BODY

When Christ went into the wilderness following His baptism, He was seemingly more alone than at any other time in His life. But He was not actually alone; He was with the Father. The purpose of fasting and communing with God for 40 days was to prepare Himself for the ministry that was to follow—readying His mind and His body, and bracing Himself for the days ahead.

Knowing that Jesus was starving due to the lengthy fast, Satan said to Him: "... *command these stones to become loaves of bread.*"

But what he was really saying was this: "Jesus, I was listening when Your Father said that You are His beloved Son in whom He is well pleased. But here You are in the desert now, and You're starving. You've been fasting all of these days, and God's not going to take care of You. Hunger is a normal and natural physical appetite. Go ahead; just turn these rocks into bread, and feed Yourself."

Satan's first temptation of Jesus was to fulfill a God-given desire, hunger, in a God-forbidden way.

Temptations of the body are sometimes called sins of the flesh. They are the promises of pleasure, satisfaction, or gain regarding the body, and can come from sex, food, alcohol, sleep, or whatever it is that satiates the flesh.

We all have natural drives and desires in our life that are God-given; sex and hunger are two examples. But Satan comes along, especially if we're hungry, angry, tired, or lonely, and he whispers, "You deserve better than this. God's not taking care of you. You need to take care of your needs. After all, they are natural, and this is normal."

And the flesh is a very powerful conduit for sin, if you yield to the power of temptation. But how often does a one-time agreement with this lie turn into a lifetime of sin? How often do people sacrifice their character and their faithfulness to God for a step outside their authentic identity in Christ to fulfill a God-given desire in a forbidden way?

TEMPTATIONS OF THE SOUL

Defeated in his temptations of the body, Satan shifted targets, and went after Jesus' mind, emotions, and will. We're not sure exactly how, but Satan and Jesus were transported to the pinnacle of the Temple Mount. But when they arrived, Satan enticed: "Remember God's promise—the angels are going to come and bear You up lest You fall and die. If You were to rely upon that protection and throw Yourself from this great height, everybody, particularly the powerful establishment, is going to believe in You. Everyone's going to see it, and they're going to know that You're God's chosen One, the Messiah. Jesus, You have the power to avoid the Cross, while proving Your deity at the same time."

Now notice how Satan reverses his strategy here, as he often does to us. In the first temptation, he was saying, God's not going to meet Your needs. But here he's saying the exact opposite—God's going to take care of You no matter what You do. Satan uses a half-truth to divert Jesus to the easy path, one avoiding the pain and loneliness of the Cross. Satan is very good at manipulating our emotions.

The temptations of the soul have to do with our personal ambitions and emotions—the approval of the world for our purchases, the "likes" of our friends (many of whom are just Facebook friends) on something we posted, and the acceptance that we long for at work (even if it means behaving in a way not in accordance with our values). Happiness, friendships, and acceptance are God-given desires, and yet Satan comes along and twists them to get us to do something wrong. Rather than trusting God's plan for our lives, Satan always tempts with the shortcut to satisfaction of our emotional and mental health needs. He shows us the easy path, knowing that the toll we will pay is one that will eventually cost us dearly.

TEMPTATIONS OF THE SPIRIT

The third temptation of Christ came in the area of spiritual allegiance.

Satan took Jesus and showed Him all the kingdoms of this world and said: "If You will just bow down and worship me, I'll give You all of this."

Now, Satan's goal has always been to be worshipped as God. Lucifer, the son of the morning, became Satan, the father of the night, because he rebelled against God in eternity past. He became the evil one because he desired worship. And he still desires to be worshipped today.

So he said to Jesus, "Look at all the glistening and glamorous kingdoms of the world. You don't need to go to the Cross. You don't need God's way. Do it my way, briefly bow down and worship me, and You can have all of this, no cost."

Notice, Jesus didn't rebuke him and say, "Satan you don't have it to give." The Bible tells us that Satan is the god of this age and the ruler of the kingdom of this world. Satan has some mighty powerful persuasive packages to offer if we will just say "yes" to him.

JACK GRAHAM

Satan is attractive; he disguises himself as an angel of light; and if Satan were to walk up to you, you would not shriek and run in terror, you would be tempted to bow down and worship him. This is what a third of the angels did, before they were cast out of heaven to live as demons.

But that is not how Satan tempts our spirit. He is far more sophisticated.

When Jesus was tested in the wilderness, He was in a barren and deserted place. When He was tempted at the temple, He was in a high and exalted place populated by the elites of the culture, yet isolated from them.

You see, the wilderness may seem barren and not being part of the "in-crowd" may seem lonely, but we actually need these seasons and places to remove the distractions of the world, draw close to God, learn to lean on Him, and gain strength from His presence. It's in these moments that we mature, and God prepares us for what's to come.

Well, we know what happened after Jesus resisted the temptations that appealed to His body, soul, and spirit. He rose to prominence—carrying out His miraculous ministry for three years, culminating at the Cross where He fulfilled all of the law and became the Savior of the world.

Just like Jesus, we will never experience personal victory

until we first overcome temptation. So we should recognize temptation as testing ground and remember it is not a sin to be tempted.

So how do we do it? How do we triumph when the test comes our way?

VICTORY OVER TEMPTATION

We deal with temptation in one of three ways: We give in to it; we try to fight it in the strength of our flesh; or we overcome it as Christ did.

Many give up and give in. But that's just not an option for us if we are children of God.

Maybe you're a new believer, or maybe you've been a believer a long time, and you're surprised that you're still dealing with some of the same stuff—the same habits, the same problems, temptations that you thought would eventually go away.

As an analogy to the sin and the consequences we have produced in our past lives, imagine if Ford Motor Company were to close down today. If Ford were to just quit making cars, you would still see Ford cars and trucks all over the highways, at least for years, because the product would still be out there.

Well, when Jesus Christ moved into our life, He shut down the production and the power of sin and judgment in our lives, but the products of sin—those old Fords—are still operating.

The thing is, we can't overcome our sinful nature and the power of temptation just by positive thinking and hoping the old sins go away.

Instead, the only way to win over temptation is to overcome it as Christ did.

So how do we replicate what He did? Look at what 1 Corinthians 10:13 says:

> *No temptation has overtaken you that is not common to man. God is faithful, and he will not let you be tempted beyond your ability, but with the temptation he will also provide the way of escape, that you may be able to endure it.*

Now, that's a wonderful promise from God's Word! So how does He provide that way of escape?

God will show us *a way out* and *a way through*. Just as you would be protective of your children, and you would do anything to keep them from falling face down, God the Father is faithful to you and to me. He will defend us and provide *a way out* and *a way through*—the exit strategy—in the face of any and all temptations.

The key is, He needs us to be **PURE**! We must:

Prepare for spiritual attack.
Undo unholy alliances.
Remember the consequences of fatal attractions.
Engage in positive, spiritual, biblical activities in our life.

These four principals can use to help us follow the path God has set out for us.

P—PREPARE FOR SPIRITUAL ATTACK.

The following are just a few Scriptures to remind us to be watchful and prepare:

> First Corinthians 10:12 says, *"Therefore let anyone who thinks that he stands take heed lest he fall."*
>
> Jesus said in Mark 14:38, *"Watch and pray that you may not enter into temptation. The spirit indeed is willing, but the flesh is weak."*
>
> Jesus taught us to pray in Matthew 6:13, *"… lead us not into temptation…."*
>
> First Peter 5:8 says, *"Be sober-minded; be watchful. Your adversary the devil prowls around like a roaring lion, seeking someone to devour."*

To be prepared for these spiritual battles, we must be

watchful and *take up the whole armor of God, that (we) may be able to withstand in the evil day, and having done all, to stand firm* (Ephesians 6:13). If we don't, we will surely become victims, rather than victors.

So, you've got the world coming at you with all of its appeal and attractiveness. You see the glimmer of the far country—the glamour of the pleasures of this world. How do you deal with that? The Bible says resist the devil and he will flee from you. But how in the world, with this giant Enemy against us, how do we simply resist?

Get your boots on; get ready to fight; and heed the call by living in simple faith!

First John 5:4–5 says:

> *For everyone who has been born of God overcomes the world. And this is the victory that has overcome the world—our faith. Who is it that overcomes the world except the one who believes that Jesus is the Son of God?*

It's the faith and trust that come from knowing Him, as the apostle Paul talked about when he said in Philippians 3:10, "… *that I may know Him and the power of his resurrection…*" If you know Him in this way, in intimate fellowship, you will be able to stand against the world.

We used to sing an old song, when I was a teenager.

> *Turn your eyes upon Jesus,*
> *Look full in His wonderful face,*
> *And the things of earth will grow strangely dim*
> *In the light of His glory and grace.*

You see, if you're not in love with Jesus the way you ought to be, it's a warning light of spiritual sickness. If you fall in love with Jesus and fully give your life to Him, the world and all of its attractions and distractions will have less and less appeal.

You will understand and desire what really matters; and not be so focused on how much money you make, how much sex you are having, or other worldly measures. If you don't walk with Jesus every day and fall in love with a life with Him, you're going to be unhappy, and temptations will always be a struggle.

U—UNDO UNHOLY ALLIANCES.

Second Corinthians 6:14 says, *"Do not be unequally yoked with unbelievers."* Verse 17 says, *"'Therefore go out from their midst, and be separate from them, says the Lord, and touch no unclean thing; then I will welcome you …'"*

In our culture, we have allowed ourselves to become linked with those things that are impure and immoral. Christians used to talk about separating from the world, but not so much anymore. Biblical separation is more positive than you might think. It's not as much about *not* doing something or isolating from the world like the monks in Greece, but more about turning from something to Someone! We turn from sin and the unholy things of the world, and positively turn to God and receive His power for living.

The fact is, there are some things that we're commanded not to do in the Christian life, and one of them is not to be unequally yoked. By sharing intimacy (physical, emotional, or spiritual) with people who are in the world, we will undoubtedly be put in positions where we will be tempted and setting ourselves up for spiritual failure.

Does that mean we are not to have friends outside the Church? Not at all, we are commanded to show love and compassion and friendliness to people who don't know Christ. We should develop relationships with people in order to share our faith with them, not seek fulfillment of our needs. God has called us to fellowship with His people, so our primary associations in life should be found there.

What about the associations we make with what we listen to and watch? I'm really surprised at some of the things people open their hearts to through their eyes. If you are not willing to separate yourself from entertainment that is unholy—movies, television, magazines—you're going to be in a constant war with sin and temptation.

Also, just as we should practice preventative medicine—exercise and healthy eating—we should practice preventative spiritual checkups. We can do that by having accountability relationships with like-minded believers.

In Jesus' name, raise the standard of your public and private associations, then attach to godly associations that will build you up and strengthen you in your faith. Find godly friends you can trust and be willing to share your heart and your life with them. Allow them to speak into your life with encouragement and correction, if necessary. It's much harder to get off track when you have someone who knows your struggles and with whom you are in regular contact.

R—REMEMBER THE CONSEQUENCES OF FATAL ATTRACTIONS

Since we have these promises, beloved, let us cleanse ourselves from every defilement of body and spirit, bringing holiness to completion in the fear of God (2 Corinthians 7:1).

One thing that keeps me walking in obedience to God is the wholesome fear of Almighty God. You see, God is a holy God, and He demands holiness in me. First Peter 1:16 says, " ... *be holy, for I am holy."* Yes, because of grace, all of our sins are forgiven. But God also holds me accountable for my life.

I think what's happened to our country in a very real sense

is that we have forgotten the fear of God.

When you are faced with temptations, remember the consequences of the various fatal attractions: a broken marriage, loss of the respect of your children, obesity, loss of employment, disease, financial debt, the loss of leadership in the Church, but most importantly the destruction of your witness and testimony for Christ.

I am not saying we should live in shame of our past failures, as we will discuss more in the next chapter, but it's important to remember the consequences of yielding to temptation, before we allow ourselves to be in a dangerous position.

E—ENGAGE IN POSITIVE, SPIRITUAL, BIBLICAL ACTIVITIES IN OUR LIFE

The best way to make sure we don't yield to temptation is to engage in positive spiritual activities.

Just as Jesus rebuked Satan's temptations with Scripture, so you should fortify your faith with the Word of God.

> *How can a young man cleanse his way? By taking heed according to Your word. With my whole heart I have sought You; Oh, let me not wander from Your commandments! Your word I have hidden in my heart that I might not sin against you* (Psalm 119:9–11, NKJV).

When we're in the Word, the power of God is at work, changing us and purifying our hearts and minds. Hide God's word in your heart. Memorize it; mark it; make it your own. Fortify your faith. How do you do that? *"So faith comes from hearing, and hearing through the word of Christ"* (Romans 10:17).

Our mind is renewed by meditating—by concentrating on holy things rather than unholy things.

> *Finally, brethren, whatever things are true, whatever things are noble, whatever things are just, whatever things are pure, whatever things are lovely, whatever things are of good report, if there is any virtue and if there is anything praiseworthy, meditate on these things* (Philippians 4:8, NKJV).

It's not just a "Don't do this; don't do that" mentality. If you decide to go on a diet to lose weight, it's important to eat the right things, not just avoid the wrong things. And if you spend your time thinking about not eating cheeseburgers, you're doing it the wrong way!

Instead, we defeat strongholds of sin in our life by being actively involved in biblical, spiritual things. We must discipline our minds, and not allow fantasies, lies, and temptations to live there. Second Corinthians 10:5 says we should *"[cast] down arguments and every high thing that exalts itself against the knowledge of God, bringing every thought into captivity to the obedience of Christ"* (NKJV).

Instead, magnify the Lord Jesus in your life. When it gets right down to it, we must have a greater love for our relationship with Jesus than anything, especially our own natural desires.

We must love Jesus with all our heart, mind, soul, and strength; and to be able to say, "Lord, I don't want to do anything in my life that will disrupt or defeat my relationship with You." When you get to this point, you will have freedom.

When we love God, the things of this world may not vanish, but they will dissipate as you grow stronger in your faith. When we magnify Jesus in our life through worship, prayer, and walking in the spirit, He enables us to stand against life's temptations of our body, soul, and spirit.

So many people sacrifice the eternal on the altars of the earthly in the temporal, and yield to temptation. But as you turn to Christ, the Word of God, and the fellowship of like-minded believers, you will turn every temptation into a triumph and every vulnerability into a victory in Jesus Christ!

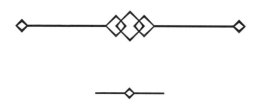

chapter nine

HELP! I'M FILLED WITH SHAME

I reserved the topic of shame as the last chapter in this book because shame can be a lingering condition for which we need help. Those who are crippled by fear; those who made poor choices under the influence of stress, anger, or addiction; those who are flattened by loneliness, grief, or depression; and those who have fallen for temptation can suffer shame.

When you consider these emotions and actions that can trigger shame, it's easy to see how many people are struggling with shame. Perhaps it's someone you know; perhaps it's someone you love; perhaps it's you.

You might think that shame is a natural and godly reaction to our sinful behavior. You might think that believers should be shameful of past sinful choices: the infidelity, the alcoholism, the dark desires, the wallowing in selfish piety, the inappropriate movies and sites viewed on the computer, the parenting failures, or the compulsive and extravagant spending on clothes.

But I want you to know that nothing is further from the truth, and nothing more directly contradicts God's Word! Does that statement sound wrong to you? Does that fly in the face of what you have been taught? This is seemingly contrary to what we have heard in our churches for years. But once we examine Scripture, I think you will embrace what I am saying, but more importantly, what the Bible says about shame.

WHAT IS SHAME?

As a clear way to explain shame, I'd like to share this personal anecdote. I was taking my young family to dinner at a burger chain in Orlando, Fla., where we were set to visit Disney World the next day. Then it happened. My daughter, Kelly, who was 9 years old at the time, was eating and spilled ketchup all over the front of her shirt. This wasn't the first time, the 10th time, but seemingly the 100th time. I had had enough. I had warned her scores of times before about being more careful and not spilling ketchup on herself, and she had done it again! I then decreed my verdict: "Kelly, you are banned from ketchup for one year." She responded with tears and pleads for mercy from the terrible judgment. Admittedly, it was not my finest hour as a parent.

Of course, by the end of the vacation, my absurd punishment had been reversed. (The cooler head of my wife, Deb, prevailed upon me.) Kelly was eating ketchup again. But my poor reaction now serves as the basis of a shared family joke. Kelly is 42 now—a beautiful, graceful mother of three who never spills ketchup. But if anyone in my family, me included, is caught with a spill stain on their shirt—whether it be ketchup, salsa, or any other dipping sauce—they are jokingly banned from that condiment for a year. And that story is a nice little anecdote to talk about shame.

When Kelly spilled the ketchup, she felt guilty. She had a moment of minor clumsiness. She wasted the all-too-precious condiment, caused a small disturbance at our otherwise pleasant meal, caused Deb and me unnecessary work and hassle in cleaning her up. And sadly, Kelly realized she might have ruined her Mickey Mouse shirt. What she felt was *guilt*.

It would have been considered *shame* had she told herself—upon spilling the ketchup and having been confronted about her condiment crime—"I am a careless child; I am not as tidy of an eater as my older brother; I have always been a ketchup spiller, and I will always be a ketchup spiller. It's just who I am, and I should stop trying to be different." But thankfully, that wasn't what she experienced.

There are several differences between guilt and shame, and the differences are critical.

Guilt is: "I did something bad. I did something wrong." Guilt comes from a wrongful act or omission.

But shame is related to our identity. Shame says: "I am bad! I am flawed!" When shame speaks, it says we are "less than" because of our sin or because of the sin of others. The addict tells himself, "I am nothing but an addict." The victim of abuse tells herself she is less than others because of what happened to her.

Dr. Ed Welch, a noted counselor, gives this definition: "Shame is the deep sense that you are inherently flawed, unacceptable and unworthy of love because of something you've done, or something done to you or something associated with you."

Guilt is felt by the individual who committed the sin. Shame is highly contagious and spreads if left unabated. The family of the alcoholic, the wife whose husband cheats on her, the church whose leader goes astray, the company whose CEO is indicted for white collar crime—all feel shame.

We can know why we feel guilty; it is objective, it can be linked to a specific time, place, and event. But shame can envelop us in our childhood, with the sufferer never understanding why he or she felt "less than." How horrible it is that so many adults feel a sense of shame for abuse—whether physical, emotional, or sexual—that was inflicted upon them in their innocence.

Shame and guilt have the same father: sin. When we feel guilt, we feel a prick of conscience and we know that we've broken one of God's commandments or done something that has been offensive to another person. When we feel shame, it is a lie from the pit of hell that we, who have been forgiven and cleansed, are somehow still dirty and tainted.

Guilt is the motivation for repentance, and shame is the deception that we can never receive redemption. God uses guilt to convict us of sin and to point us to the Cross for redemption and restoration. God never uses shame.

Shame will destroy you physically, mentally, emotionally, psychologically and, yes, spiritually. Shame will cripple your recovery. Shame will be a bitter legacy for your children. So, let's deal with this now.

WHAT DOES THE BIBLE SAY ABOUT SHAME?

In Genesis when Adam and Eve ate of the Tree of Knowledge of Good and Evil, they violated God's only law at the time. In His kindness and protection for them, He expressly told them to keep one simple rule. He knew if they ate of the fruit of this tree, their soul would be changed. They would suddenly begin to act in self-sufficiency rather than close, intimate communion with and dependence on their Maker. He also knew that this new awareness of "self" would ultimately lead to shame. Shame is one of the biggest obstacles, even to this day, between people and God. Adam and Eve felt shortchanged because they believed a lie—a lie that many who suffer from shame fall for every day, minute by minute. This lie was that who they were, as God made them, was not sufficient.

It wasn't that they wanted to live a life tempted by sin. No, they first believed the lie that God was withholding something from them. They no longer believed that what He had created in them was sufficient. So, they ate the forbidden fruit. And at that moment, guilt and shame were ushered into their existence. The guilt came immediately and quickly, but the shame lingered far longer. Out of guilt, they tried to hide from God; out of shame, they recognized their nakedness and tried to cover themselves. What God had intended for them was a life of wholeness, full of everything they needed. A life without shame where they were exposed, real, with no physical adornments to "complete them." But when they sinned, the shame overtook them and resulted in their recognizing their nakedness.

But here is the thing that I love about this story. Yes, God pronounced a punishment for their sin. Yes, they would be exiled from the Garden, childbirth would be painful, and man would have to toil all the days of his life in the soil. But God did something for them out of total love and merciful kindness. He fashioned clothes for them. He covered them!

It was the shame they carried that caused them to hide and recognize their nakedness—their new sinful nature and identity. And what did God do? An animal was sacrificed to provide a covering for the shame they felt.

The same love and kindness are evident throughout the Old Testament. The innocent, unblemished Lamb would be sacrificed to remove the sin and guilt from Israel. The scapegoat would then be released into the wild to carry away the shared and personal shames of the nation.

The cycle of sin, shame, and sacrifice continued for centuries until God provided a permanent solution for cleansing all of humanity of sin, guilt, and shame. When Christ died on the Cross, He was the sacrificial Lamb. His precious blood became our permanent covering, turning our soiled wool into pure white. But not only was He the unblemished Lamb, He was the scapegoat which forever took away the shame of all those who call themselves by His name. Shame had been defeated.

He not only died *for* sin, He died *as* sin. He became sin for us. He became shame for us. He died on the Cross, in nakedness, in agony, and in blood. He died exposed for the whole world to see! He took our shame when He took our sin. He removed our sin and shame, *"as far as the east is from the west"* (Psalm 103:12), and He *"will cast all our sins into the depths of the sea"* (Micah 7:19).

The Christian life is a changed life! *"Therefore, if anyone is in Christ, he is a new creation. The old has passed away; behold, the new has come"* (2 Corinthians 5:17). You and I are changed by God!

We often quote Romans 8:38–39: *"For I am sure that neither death nor life, nor angels nor rulers, nor things present nor things to come, nor powers, nor height nor depth, nor anything else in all creation, will be able to separate us from the love of God in Christ Jesus our Lord."*

If you're a believer living in shame, know that your past, present, or future sins, or the sins of others can't keep you from the love of God in Christ Jesus our Lord, either! *"I have been crucified with Christ. It is no longer I who live, but Christ who lives in me..."* (Galatians 2:20).

You don't have to live in guilt; live in grace. You don't have to live in shame; live in salvation. What incredible freedom we have in knowing that He has seen our nakedness, our true identity; and He has said that we no longer need to hide from His wrath or cover ourselves. Because He was a sufficient sacrifice for all our sins. He has cleansed us from all unrighteousness.

HOW DO WE RELEASE THE BONDS OF SHAME?

So how do we deal with the shame that permeates our body, soul, and spirit? We begin with a *request for forgiveness*, we *receive forgiveness*, and we *release forgiveness*. If we have already been born again, we get rooted in our true identity in Christ, and we experience empathy and fellowship with other believers.

We must request forgiveness.
We must start with sin itself. First ours, and later we will deal with those who have sinned against us.

- **What is sin?**

There is so much brokenness in our world, nation, and families because of the problem of sin and all the resultant misery that is on the heels of sin. Clearly, the world wants to rebrand sin, but what does the Bible say about sin?

Well, number one, sin is defiant. The Bible describes sin as lawlessness and rebellion against almighty God. Sin is a fist in the face of a holy God.

Sin is also described in the Bible as disobedience when

we break the commandments of God, whether it be the Ten Commandments or the explanation of the Ten Commandments that we find in the Bible.

Sin is defilement, something that corrupts and is toxic to our body, soul, or spirit.

Sin is a death dealing disease. *"For the wages of sin is death..."* (Romans 6:23). And like cancer cells, you either aggressively kill the sin, or the sin will kill you.

Sin is deceitful. The price of sin is always a hidden, heavy cost.

Sin is destructive ... not only to us, but to those all around us.

And finally, sin is devilish. First John 3:8 tells us: *"Whoever makes a practice of sinning is of the devil, for the devil has been sinning from the beginning...."* The "original sin" was not Adam's, but Lucifer's.

- **All have sinned.**

The problem is the sin that is within every person who is born on the face of this earth. *"... for all have sinned and fall short of the glory of God"* (Romans 3:23). Jesus said in Matthew 15:19, *"For out of the heart come evil thoughts, murder, adultery, sexual immorality, theft, false witness, slander."* We have all sinned! I don't think I need to expand upon that any more than to clarify one point.

• What is sanctification?

When God saved you, He did not take away the possibility of sin in your life. And certainly, there is within the Christian a new nature that resists sin, but we do sin. Somebody said, "You know, when God saves us, He doesn't fix us so that we can't sin anymore. He just fixes us so that we can't sin and enjoy it anymore!"

Sin is a serious matter. To the unbeliever, it is serious because it means destruction, judgment, hell, and damnation. To the believer, it means broken fellowship with God. When we accept Christ as our Savior, all of our sin is forgiven, and our guilt is removed. That is *justification*. And though the relationship with God is secure in Jesus Christ, when sin occurs, our relationship can be distorted. When you receive Jesus Christ as your Lord and Savior, you're called upon to live the Gospel in your daily affairs, a constant cleaning of your body, soul, and spirit. This is called *sanctification*; we are always coming clean. And in order to be sanctified, we must *request forgiveness*; we will *receive forgiveness*; and we must *release forgiveness*.

When we fail—and we do fail—none of this is a surprise to the Lord; none of it. Jesus wasn't surprised that Peter failed; He predicted it; He prophesied it. But when you fail, rather than falling back into the past of defeat, and living there in shame and regret for the rest of your days, you can fall forward into the grace of God!

First John 1:9 says, *"If we confess our sins, he is faithful and just to forgive us our sins and to cleanse us from all unrighteousness."* Confession means "to agree with" or "to say the same thing as." In other words, when I am confessing my sin, I am agreeing with God and what God says and not what I say. I confess it by saying, "God, this is wrong, and You are right. This doesn't need to be a part of my life."

There are two attitudes that every believer must possess in requesting forgiveness:

One is the attitude of honesty. No hiding, no alibis, no excuses. Proverbs 28:13 says, *"Whoever conceals his transgressions will not prosper, but he who confesses and forsakes them will obtain mercy."*

We must also confess with humility. Ego is the enemy of forgiveness.

And so, requesting forgiveness means that we honestly, humbly, come before God and ask Him to forgive us. And that moves me to the second element of dealing with our sin to receive sanctification, receiving forgiveness.

We must receive forgiveness.

Over and over again, the Word of God promises pardon to all who ask.

When Christ died upon the Cross, our debt was paid in full; freely, fully. Jesus cancelled all of our sins and made it possible for us to receive the forgiveness of God. God almighty, offended by our sin, is now releasing love and forgiveness to us through the Cross.

But the problem is, for some, it seems impossible to forget sins. You are living with skeletons in your closet, and the emotional drain and pain is haunting you. You say, "Well, I can't forget those things." That's why the Scripture says the Word of God cleanses us. And as you bathe yourself in the Word of God, you are able to forgive yourself.

The great British preacher Charles Haddon Spurgeon said, "As far as God is concerned, your sin has ceased to be. He laid it on Jesus Christ, your substitute, and he took it and bore the penalty of it—nay the thing itself; he as your scapegoat, carried your sin right away, and it is lost in the wilderness of forgetfulness."

In Micah 7:18, Scripture tells us God delights to give mercy, even though we've sinned again and again and again and again. God almighty longs to forgive you and extend His unfathomable, unimaginable grace.

Christian, please hear this; please understand this. So many of you are living with the fear that somehow God is going to "get you" for something that happened long ago. It's forgotten. *"But to all who did receive him, who believed in his name, he gave the right to become children of God …"* (John 1:12). You are now the child of a Father whose love and mercy surpasses all understanding. Receive and rest in His forgiveness. You've been changed by the power of Jesus Christ. Ask Him and receive it. As Spurgeon said, "You are a great sinner, but he is a greater Saviour."

We must release forgiveness.

In order to fully deal with sin, we must release forgiveness. When He taught us to pray, Jesus said, *"… forgive us our debts, as we also have forgiven our debtors"* (Matthew 6:12). Forgiveness is to be understood in light of our willingness to forgive others. Now, Jesus is not saying that we are forgiven on the basis of our willingness to forgive others. That would be *works*. But Jesus is saying simply this: People who are forgiven are forgiving. People who recognize they have been relieved of such great debt let go of hostility, resentments, bitterness, and yes, in turn, shame.

For believers struggling with the shame of their sins, applying daily the principles of sanctification in receiving forgiveness is critical.

But for those believers who suffer shame as the result of

the sin of others—whether it's sin committed against you or shame you feel because of your relationship with another person—releasing forgiveness is vital.

If you are living in the past with the abuses and the offenses perpetrated by your parents, your partner, your pastor or priest, or your business associate, it seems like justice in holding that hurt in. Somehow, we think in the retaliation of our spirit that we're hurting the other person, but in reality, we're only hurting ourselves.

The shame we carry for what others may have done to us, however hurtful, spiteful, vile, wicked, or criminal, must be dealt with. It should never be tolerated in any form or any fashion. It must be dealt with spiritually, and should be dealt with through church discipline, civil courts, and in the criminal justice system if warranted.

But regardless, you must forgive those who have hurt you. A bitter spirit is fertile ground for Satan to work. Hatred, resentment, anger, and chronic criticism are destroyers of the body, soul, and spirit. And when you hold resentment toward someone, you're just holding yourself hostage. It is such a release … it is such a freedom … to let all of that shame go, to turn it loose and to forgive as you have been forgiven.

You say, "Pastor, you have no idea how that person

abused me." You're absolutely right. I don't. And there are some unimaginable atrocities and abuses you may have experienced, and nobody can understand it but you and one other person ... Jesus.

For when Jesus was tortured and crucified, He took on your sin and shame. He cried out: *"Father, forgive them, for they know not what they do"* (Luke 23:34). Put yourself at the foot of the Cross, Christian. That's what it means to take up your cross and follow Jesus. It's not always easy to be a follower of Jesus Christ, but it's always best. And let the love of Jesus Christ flow through you. Forgiveness is possible for us and for others because of the Cross.

And remember, the goal of forgiving someone else is not just so that we'll feel better, or reconciliation with the offender, if that is possible, but more importantly, sanctification.

When Peter was forgiven and restored after he repented having denied Christ—three times he denied Him—Jesus gave him the opportunity to confess Him three times, saying: "Feed my lambs." "Tend my sheep." "Feed my sheep." In other words, "You're forgiven. Now extend My grace and My love to others." Forgiven, we forgive.

We embrace our true identity in Christ.
Shame lies to us and says we are unacceptable, and our

nakedness, our authentic redeemed self is dirty, disgraceful, and distances us from others and God. Shame leads so many to sin or keeps them in their sin. Shame is the serpent that coyly whispers that we are not sufficient because of our past sins and even worse because of the sins of others against us. Such thinking is a lie that the Great Deceiver wants you to believe because he knows shame can keep you in your sin and robs Christ of the victory He won at the Cross.

It is God's love that liberates us and sets us free from the power of sin and shame. *"There is therefore now no condemnation for those who are in Christ Jesus"* (Romans 8:1). And He has removed our sin and shame *"as far as the east is from the west"* (Psalm 103:12). But when the days are tough, when anger, stress, temptations, or addictive patterns of behavior rise and attempt to ensure, shame will rise and lie to us about our identity and tell us that we are not sufficient.

No! Believe not the lies of the Enemy, believe what God says about you! You are a child of God! You are fulfilled in Jesus Christ! You are forgiven! You are cleansed! You are healed! You are redeemed! You are restored! No more shame! Leave that behind you and live in the grace and the covering and the cleansing that Christ provides by His precious blood.

You were made *by* God and *for* God! And He is the only One who knows you intimately.

God knows every scar and every sin you have committed. Yet, He looks at you through the lens of your faith in Christ and says, "You're mine!" There's no amount of human reason that can explain a love such as that. So instead of focusing on your past shortcomings or feelings of insufficiency, see yourself as God sees you in Christ: holy, blameless, and acceptable to Him.

We show empathy and we fellowship with believers.

> The Lord is very ready to forgive: it is the church that is unmerciful sometimes, but not the Master: he is ever willing to receive us when we come to him, and to blot out our transgression.... Just so does your heavenly Father wait to catch you up, and to press you to his bosom and say, "I have loved thee with an everlasting love."
>
> —Charles Haddon Spurgeon in his sermon, "God's Fatherly Pity"

Churches such as those in Spurgeon's Victorian-era England spoke of sin, guilt, and shame continually, but so little was devoted to grace. No wonder Spurgeon's preaching was so popular. It was always uncompromisingly confrontational with sin, but always pointing to the Good News.

The subject of shame is something rarely discussed in

churches. Too often, shame has been bound with guilt, and never directly addressed. But in recent years, churches have been more intentional about addressing shame and ministering to those filled with shame. And much of this came about because of the work of secular counselors, therapists, psychologists, and psychiatrists.

Dr. Brené Brown, of the University of Houston, has devoted her research and her large media platform to the subject of shame, calling it "the most primitive human emotion." And given what we know about Adam and Eve, I tend to agree.

Dr. Brown shares that "shame needs three things to grow exponentially in our lives: secrecy, silence, and judgment." She reports, "Shame depends on me buying into the belief that I'm alone," so an antidote is sharing your shame with someone who will listen to you with empathy.

I totally agree with this antidote, but I would add that we also need to deal with any underlying sinful behavior, through the necessary repentance, forgiveness of others, and clinging to our identity in Christ as we have discussed above.

The generally accepted definition of empathy is the ability to recognize, understand, and share the thoughts and feelings of another person.

And I am encouraged about the great work being done in

the Church today on encouraging a culture of empathy by providing counseling, life recovery ministries, or groups for those who struggle with the emotional and mental health issues we have discussed in this book, and ministers and leaders publicly talking about their struggles.

And that is how it should be, and that is how the Church was founded.

Recall Simon Peter's miserable failure in denying Christ three times. Peter was an intimate of the Lord. Peter saw all the miracles of Christ. Peter heard firsthand the teachings. Peter saw the changed lives. But what did he do, in his cowardice and shame in his identity? He denied Christ.

If any sin warrants a lifetime of shame, it would have been Peter's sin.

Simon Peter failed miserably, but he moved past his grievous errors and went on to perform miracles and became the powerful preacher at Pentecost and the leader of the first-century church. How did all of this happen when he could have understandably spent a lifetime wallowing in shame?

He confessed his sin; he repented; he was restored with Christ; he fully reconciled with Christ and the disciples. And he did this openly and honestly. Later in his writings, Peter would relate this shameful episode in his life. He would talk about it. And you know why Simon was willing to talk about his shame, the terrible defeat in his life when "The Rock" crumbled?

Because he was able to say, "Look what Jesus did for me! When I failed, He didn't fail me. When I denied, He didn't deny me. When I crumbled, He lifted me! When I felt worthless, He showed me my true, invaluable identity." Jesus never mistook the moment for the man. So Simon Peter became that powerful witness for Christ.

FINAL THOUGHTS ON SHAME

Most of us know of the legendary football player and sportscaster Pat Summerall. Pat was the unmistakably steadfast voice of the National Football League for more than 20 years as well as providing play-by-play for the U.S. Open and The Masters.

But what you may not know is that Pat was a recovering alcoholic. He wrote about this in his wonderful memoir titled *Summerall: On and Off the Air*. For years, Pat had a major problem with alcohol that resulted in a hedonistic lifestyle. And when his daughter confronted him about the shame that she felt because of his drinking, Pat knew he needed help. So he entered the Betty Ford Clinic where he learned to overcome his addiction, but he also began to read the Bible. And he soon found that "missing ingredient" he had been trying to find. He found his Savior!

Jesus came and filled the void that Pat had tried to fill with alcohol for so long. Jesus emptied Pat of the shame he felt, so he could share his past struggle and help others with their struggles.

I was blessed to be Pat's pastor and friend. He was such an encouragement to me and all who knew him. In 2013, I was honored to preach at Pat's funeral and share the Good News of the Gospel that had transformed Pat's life with many people who might never have otherwise set foot in a church.

In his book, Pat wrote, "Now I revel in the redeeming grace that God has bestowed upon me."

If you struggle with shame, revel in the redeeming grace God has given you, embrace your identity in Christ, and honestly and humbly extend His love and yours to others!

Final Thoughts

GRATITUDE—THE HEALTHIEST OF EMOTIONS

In this book, we've been talking about the various mental and emotional health needs in peoples' lives—whether it be stress, anger, grief, loneliness, addiction, anxiety, depression, or shame. And in preparing this book, it occurred to me that if a person wants to be spiritually, emotionally, and even physically healthy, there is an *attitude of gratitude* that fuels it all.

The healthiest human emotion, according to Hans Selye, a psychologist and the father of the famous stress study, is gratitude. Think about it. If you are blessed and you know that you are blessed, it counteracts ... it is the antidote to toxic emotion in our lives.

The Scriptures are filled with praises, worship, and thanksgiving to the Lord. It's all the way through the Bible. *"I will bless the LORD at all times; his praise shall continually be in my mouth"* (Psalm 34:1). *"... give thanks in all circumstances; for this is the will of God in Christ Jesus for you*" (1 Thessalonians 5:18).

So often, gratitude is the missing ingredient in our lives, and even in our prayers.

You remember those 10 lepers in Luke 17? Jesus healed all of them, but only one came back to say thank you. When we read that, we might think to ourselves, "Well, I know I would have come back to say thank you," and maybe that's true. But think about that, only 10 percent of those lepers healed from a devastating lifelong disease came back to say, "Thank You, Jesus."

I imagine for all the things that He's done for us, we probably only say thank you to God about 10 percent of the time. That means we are likely to give thanks for only one out of 10 of the blessings of God. Grateful prayer has a profound impact in so many ways and the ability to say, "Thank You, Lord," is one of the greatest blessings in the life of a Christian.

Ruth Graham, Billy Graham's wife, said this: "Gratitude dissolves doubt, reinforces faith, and restores joy. You would worry less if you praised God more!"

Gratitude destroys discontent, dissatisfaction, and discomfort, often the sources of fears which fuel our discontent.

When I was emotionally struggling following my cancer diagnosis, I was advised by a wise counsellor to write down my thoughts, my fears, and my blessings every day. That prescription, coupled with prayer and sharing my struggle with others, enabled me to clarify things. It was the help I needed. I would advise you to keep a journal, and if nothing else, write down two or three of the blessings of God upon your life every day. It's a proven antidote when we are in need of help.

"Count your blessings; name them one by one" is an old, old song, but it's an ever-new treatment when we are in need of help.

As Christians, we should count our blessings; we should be grateful in all circumstances.

In Romans 1:21, we are told that ingratitude is the mark of the unbeliever. *"For although they knew God, they did not honor him as God or give thanks to him...."*

The mark of a believer is thanksgiving and gratitude. We have grateful hearts because of what Christ has done for us. We enter into the presence of God with thanksgiving and praise.